CHRIST'S
DEITY

CHRIST'S DEITY

THE DEITY OF THE LORD JESUS CHRIST; TRUTH, MYTH AND CHALLENGES.

ANNIE NGANA-MUNDEKE (PH.D).

iUniverse, Inc.
Bloomington

CHRIST'S DEITY
THE DEITY OF THE LORD JESUS CHRIST;
TRUTH, MYTH AND CHALLENGES.

iUniverse books may be ordered through booksellers or by contacting:

iUniverse
1663 Liberty Drive
Bloomington, IN 47403
www.iuniverse.com
1-800-Authors (1-800-288-4677)

ISBN: 978-1-4620-3788-9 (sc)
ISBN: 978-1-4620-3789-6 (ebk)

Printed in the United States of America

iUniverse rev. date: 04/18/2012

THE TABLE OF CONTENTS

In the beginning was the Word, and the Word was with God, and the Word was God. ²He was with God in the beginning.

³Through him all things were made; without him nothing was made that has been made. ⁴In him was life, and that life was the light of men. ⁵The light shines in the darkness, but the darkness has not understood[a] it [John 1:1-5].

DEDICATION

To the Lord Jesus Christ, My Creator; Our Creator.

ACKNOWLEDGEMENTS

I thank my Lord and my God, Lord Jesus Christ for His love and for His help. I thank my parents, my brothers, my sisters, and my friends for their supports.

I also thank all preachers who believe in the Lord Jesus Christ and who have preached or have written about Christ's Deity. My special thanks go to Dr. Tim Keller, the senior pastor of the Redeemer Presbyterian Church in Manhattan, New York City, USA. I also thank my former Sunday school teacher, Frederick A. Eisenaman for his preaching and for recommending iUniverse publisher company.

NOTES FROM THE WRITER

When discussing the issue concerning God, it is important to know that God exists and He is our Creator. Also, it is important to note that God speaks to His people and He does so in many ways. God is infinite, God cannot be limited. God speaks to His people in numerous ways among which his divine word, the Scriptures, the inspired word of God. God also speaks to His people through dreams and through visions as we read in Scriptures, the breathed word of God:

All Scripture is God-breathed and is useful for teaching, rebuking, correcting and training in righteousness, so that the man of God may be thoroughly equipped for every good work [2 Timothy 3:16-17]. The word of God is powerful and the word of God is truth: [17] Sanctify them by[d] the truth; your word is truth [John 17:17]. God speaks to his people through His divine word in the Holy Bible. In Scriptures, we read that God exists and He is our Creator. If God exists and that He is our Creator, we then need to know the really name of God. When God met Moses in the bush, God told Moses that His name is "I AM WHO I AM," as we read in the Old Testament, more precisely, in the Book of Exodus 3:14.

Now, later, in the New Testament, the LORD Jesus Christ made a statement that He is "the Great I AM":

Very truly I tell you," Jesus answered, "before Abraham was born, I am!" [59] At . . . . grounds [John 8:58].

From these two statements, we learn that there is Only One God, the Great I AM. Keeping this in mind, we need to seek further in the Scriptures to learn about the Great I AM and the prophecies about the Divine Messiah. These names and several others bring some light to our understanding of the Only One God, Our Creator and Savior, the LORD Jesus Christ. Although some scholars are skeptical and refuse to see the connection between God's revelation of His name as the great I AM to Moses and the claim the LORD Jesus Christ made later, teaching that before Abraham was, He IS, it is very important to ponder why the Pharisees and the chief priests wanted to kill the Lord Jesus when He made this statement. Similarly, when the LORD called Himself the Son of Man, there were reactions and the Pharisees protested and wanted to kill Him:

> [30] I and the Father are one."

> [31] Again his Jewish opponents picked up stones to stone him,

> [32] but Jesus said to them, "I have shown you many good works from the Father. For which of these do you stone me?"

> [33] "We are not stoning you for any good work," they replied, "but for blasphemy, because you, a mere man, claim to be God [John 10:30-33].

It is really important to believe who the Lord Jesus Christ Himself says He is because God does not lie. The Lord Jesus Christ states that He is the truth and the life and the way to the father: Jesus answered, "I am the way and the truth and the life. No one comes to the Father except through me[John 14:16]. It is very important to consider this statement by the Lord. To know a person, it is important to listen to the person's own testimony. The Lord taught about His Deity and He warned that if we do not believe what He said He is, we would perish [John 8:24].

SYNOPSIS

Christ's Deity is an issue of heated debate that carries the truth and that raises challenges. What is the truth about Christ's Deity? Is the Lord Jesus Christ God, the Creator Who created the heavens and the earth, the Creator of the universe? Above all does God even exist, and because He does, did He come to earth in a form of a Human Being and was called Immanuel, and Lord Jesus Christ?

What is the truth and who tells the truth? Where can we find the truth and what should we do with the truth? To answer these questions and many others, we need to examine Scriptures because they are the breathed word of God [2 Timothy 3:16]. Scriptures teach that God exists and that God created the universe: ¹ In the beginning God created the heavens and the earth. ² Now the earth was [a] formless and empty, darkness was over the surface of the deep, and the Spirit of God was hovering over the waters [Genesis 1:1-2].

But, who is this God, the Creator of the heavens and the earth, is He the Lord Jesus Christ? What is the truth? Who knows the truth and where can we find the truth about the Almighty God, our Creator, the Creator of the universe? What does the Lord Jesus Christ teach about creation and about Himself? Does the Lord Jesus Christ ever say that He is God the Creator?

Christ's Deity is a matter of life and death, truth and challenges. The Lord states that, if we don't believe, we will perish:

²⁴ I told you that you would die in your sins; if you do not believe that I am he, you will indeed die in your sins" [John 8:24].

It is important to ask these questions to find some answers because one day, each of us will have to answer them, one way or the other, especially on the Judgment Day, because there will be a Judgment Day as the Lord Jesus Christ taught [Matthew 25:31-46].

Scriptures teach that God exists, He is our Creator and that there is Only One God. When the Lord Jesus Christ came to earth to minister, Scriptures teach that the Lord raised the dead, He healed the sick, He forgave sins, He was worshipped and He accepted worship, but we know that God does not share His glory. How come the Lord Jesus Christ accepted worship from angels, from demons, from His disciples and from peoples as we read in the Scriptures? Scriptures teach in many circumstances that the Lord Jesus Christ is worshipped. Could the Lord Jesus Christ be God, our Creator?

Who do you think the Lord Jesus Christ Is?

Christ' Deity: The Deity of the Lord Jesus Christ; Truth, Myth and Challenges addresses a serious issue of life and death, a challenging issue of ages, a historical issue that has *caused divisions*, that issue is the Deity of the Lord Jesus Christ and his claim that He is God, Our Creator, the Creator of the universe.

First, Christ's Deity is a serious issue of life and death because it is an issue which is related to life and death as Christ Himself says that he who believes in Him will never die: *"Jesus said to her, "I am the resurrection and the life. He who believes in me* will live, even though he dies" [John 11:25]; Elsewhere, The Lord Jesus Christ says that He gives eternal life:

> Whoever eats my flesh and drinks my blood has eternal life, and I will raise him up at the last day [John 6:54].

Also, the Lord says that He is the bread of life:

Jesus said to them, "I tell you the truth, it is not Moses who has given you the bread from heaven, but it is my Father who gives you the true bread from heaven. 33For the bread of God is he who comes down from heaven and gives life to the world." [John 6:32-33].

Further, in the same book of John and in the same chapter, the Lord expends and explains that He gives eternal Life:

"This is the bread that came down from heaven. Your forefathers ate manna and died, but he who feeds on this bread will live forever" [John 6:58].

In other circumstances, The Lord Jesus Christ says, "if you do not believe that I am he who I say that I am, you will die in your sins":

²⁴I told you that you would die in your sins; if you do not believe that I am the one I claim to be,[a] you will indeed die in your sins." [John 8:24].

In addition, the Lord Jesus Christ states: Because I live, you will also live [John 14:19].

Another important passage to consider about the Lord Jesus' claim about Himself is the passage where the LORD says that He is the way, the Truth and Life and that no one goes to the Father except through Him: ⁶Jesus answered, "I am the way and the truth and the life. No one comes to the Father except through me. ⁷If you really knew me, you would know[b] my Father as well. From now on, you do know him and have seen him" [John 14:6-7].

There is Only One God as Scriptures teach:

⁴ Hear, O Israel: The LORD our God, the LORD is one. [a] ⁵ Love the LORD your God with all your heart and with all your soul and with all your strength [Deuteronomy 6:4].

More important is that the Lord Jesus Christ teaches that there is Only One God:

²⁹ "The most important one," *answered Jesus, "is this: 'Hear, O Israel: The Lord our God, the Lord is one.*[c] ³⁰ Love the Lord your God with all your heart and with all your soul and with all your mind and with all your strength.'[f] ³¹ The second is this: 'Love

your neighbor as yourself.'[g] There is no commandment greater than these."

³² "Well said, teacher," the man replied. "You are right in saying that God is one and there is no other but him. ³³ To love him with all your heart, with all your understanding and with all your strength, and to love your neighbor as yourself is more important than all burnt offerings and sacrifices [Mark 12:29-33].

Also, important to consider in the discussions about Christ's Deity is the LORD's claim that He and the Father are One: *I and the Father are one*" [John 10:30]. This statement by our Lord raised tension from the audience and they wanted to kill Him [John 10:30-33]. These few passages and several others clarify the fact that Christ's Deity is an issue of life and death.

Second, Christ's Deity is a challenging issue because it challenges the mind without precedence; there is no issue that has challenged the human's mind as the issue of Christ's Deity. The fact of believing that God became Man and He lived among His peoples challenges many minds even today. Christ's Deity is a challenging issue of ages because the thought that the Lord Jesus Christ is God, our Creator, challenges the mind more than any issue a man has ever faced. Despite the challenges of life and all obstacles we face, Christ's Deity challenges the mind more because it is related to life and death, to salvation and to eternal life.

Third, Christ's Deity is an issue of ages; Christ's Deity has caused division among believers and even among non-believers for ages. Since His earthly ministry of three years and half, Christ's Deity caused division among believers. While many accepted Christ and called Him Messiah, the Anointed One, other rejected Christ as Messiah, they protested, they doubted and they affirmed that nothing good could come out of Nazareth:

Nazareth! Can anything good come from there?" Nathanael asked. "Come and see," said Philip [John 1:46].

Many people were still waiting for the Messiah; they were waiting for the Messiah despite the fulfillment of the Scriptures before their own eyes. Many rejected Christ and denied His Deity back then. Christ's Deity is an issue of ages as we have just mentioned and that has caused divisions. There are also circumstances when many left the Lord Jesus Christ when He taught about His Deity. Since His coming to earth, many have challenged His Deity, many faced challenges and had a hard time accepting that God became Man and lived among men as His name indicates, "Immanuel," God with us as we read in the Scriptures, the divine inspired word of God, in the Old Testament and in the New Testament:

- The New Testament:

   [Matthew 1:21]. The New Testament.

- The Old Testament:

   [Isaiah 7:14]. This passage is from the Old Testament.

Other passages that reveal Christ's Deity include the following:

   [Isaiah 8:10].

   [Isaiah 9:6].

   [Isaiah 9:7].

All these passages from Scriptures teach that the Lord Jesus Christ is God. Now, because Scriptures teach that the Lord Jesus Christ is called Immanuel, God with us [Matthew 1:21]; Mighty God, Everlasting God and Prince of Peace [Isaiah 9:6], can we conclude that God exists, He is our Creator and that His name is Jesus Christ? WHO IS this Triune God, the Father, the Son and the Holy Spirit?

Furthermore, several passages from Scriptures clearly indicate that the Lord Jesus Christ is God Our Creator. Among those are the passages of John 1:1-5, Colossians[I:1-15] and Isaiah 6:9 as we read:

- In the beginning was the Word, and the Word was with God, and the Word was God. [2] He was with God in the beginning. [3] Through him all things were made; without him nothing was made that has been made. [4] In him was life, and that life was the light of all mankind. [5] The light shines in the darkness, and the darkness has not overcome[a] it [John 1:1-5].

- [15]The Son is the image of the invisible God, the firstborn over all creation. [16] For in him all things were created: things in heaven and on earth, visible and invisible, whether thrones or powers or rulers or authorities; all things have been created through him and for him. [17] He is before all things, and in him all things hold together. [18] And he is the head of the body, the church; he is the beginning and the firstborn from among the dead, so that in everything he might have the supremacy. [19] For God was pleased to have all his fullness dwell in him, [20] and through him to reconcile to himself all things, whether things on earth or things in heaven, by making peace through his blood, shed on the cross[Colossians 1:1-15].

- [6]For to us a child is born,
    to us a son is given,
    and the government will be on his shoulders.
  And he will be called
    Wonderful Counselor, Mighty God,
    Everlasting Father, Prince of Peace [Isaiah 9:6].

God of the Old Testament is God of the New Testament as Scripture teach: There is Only One God [Deuteronomy 4:6 Mark 12:29]. God wants us to reason with Him. There is nothing wrong for one to try to find answers. God allows us to ask questions and wait for Him to give us answers. Scriptures teach that we need to pray and ask [Matthew 7:7; Luke 11:9]. With such a challenging issue as Christ's Deity, no one should be blamed for questioning, for challenging and for seeking answers.

INTRODUCTION

In the beginning was the Word, and the Word was with God, and the Word was God. ²He was with God in the beginning.

³Through him all things were made; without him nothing was made that has been made. ⁴In him was life, and that life was the light of men. ⁵The light shines in the darkness, but the darkness has not understood[a] it [John 1:1-5].

The discussion about God's existence, God's nature and God's creation is powerful and challenging; powerful because God is powerful and challenging because God's ways are not men's ways as we read in the Scriptures:

⁸ "For my thoughts are not your thoughts,
neither are your ways my ways,"
declares the LORD.

⁹ "As the heavens are higher than the earth,
so are my ways higher than your ways
and my thoughts than your thoughts.

¹⁰ As the rain and the snow
come down from heaven,
and do not return to it
without watering the earth
and making it bud and flourish,
so that it yields seed for the sower and bread for the eater,

¹¹ So is my word that goes out from my mouth:
It will not return to me empty,
but will accomplish what I desire
and achieve the purpose for which I sent it. [Isaiah 55:8-9].

Scriptures are the breathed word of God: [16] All Scripture is God-breathed and is useful for teaching, rebuking, correcting and training in righteousness, [2 Timothy 3:16]. The word of God is powerful and the word of God is truth, therefore, the power and the truth that are found in the word of God raise challenges to the human mind and generate serious discussions and heated debates, especially with such topics as Christ's Deity or the Deity of the Lord Jesus Christ, His nature, His deeds and His wonders.

The nature of the Lord Jesus Christ as God and as Man at the same time; or 100% God and 100% Man raises challenges that fascinate the human mind. Christ's Deity is a challenging issue of centuries that has been appealing and that has separated people as some did not understand who the LORD Jesus Christ really Is.

The discussion about God's existence and God's nature, and God's creation is powerful, challenging and informative at the same time; powerful because the issue is about the powerful God and challenging because the word of God can challenge one's mind as one cannot deny the truth and the power of the word of God. The word of God is truth and truth is powerful: [17] Sanctify them by[d] the truth; your word is truth [John 17:17]. When one reads the word of God, one needs to either accept the truth of the word of God and obey God and decide to make peace with God or one needs to choose to doubt God, to reject the truth of the word of God, to disobey God, and to live with consequences, that is to be separated from God for eternity: [John 6:54]. When all these thoughts are crossing one's mind it becomes challenging. More often the mind is overwhelmed. But the will of God is that everyone be saved because after the Fall of Man, God became Man to save His people from sin: [Matthew 1, 21-1:23].

But who is this God of the Bible, Who is loving and caring, one may ask. Who is God Almighty? What is His real Name? From the Book of Genesis to the Book of Revelation, there is mention of the Almighty God, the Creator of the universe who created the heaven and the earth and who created man in His image [Genesis 1:27]. Scripture teach us that God of the Bible Is the Only True God for there is Only God. In addition, Scriptures teach that God of the Bible is Holy, He is omnipresent, He is omniscient and He is omnipotent. He is Jehovah, the Great I AM.

Bearing this powerful truth in mind, Scriptures also teach us that God came to earth in a form of man. God took on Flesh, He lived among men, He was worshipped and He performed miracles [John 1:1-14]. This is a challenge, a remarkable obstacle that one can easily stumble upon as it is difficult to comprehend that God became MAN and the fullness of God dwelt in ONE MAN, the Lord Jesus Christ who is 100% God and 100% Man. The very fact that God became MAN causes many to stumble just as we read in Scriptures in the Book of First Peter [1 Peter 2:6-8]:

> ⁶ For in Scripture it says:

> "See, I lay a stone in Zion,
> a chosen and precious cornerstone,
> and the one who trusts in him
> will never be put to shame."[b]

> ⁷ Now to you who believe, this stone is precious. But to those who do not believe,

> "The stone the builders rejected
> has become the cornerstone,"[c]

> ⁸ and,

> "A stone that causes people to stumble
> and a rock that makes them fall."[d]

A closer look at the Scriptures reveals that Christ has the supremacy and Christ created everything:

> The Son is the image of the invisible God, the firstborn over all creation. ¹⁶ For in him all things were created: things in heaven and on earth, visible and invisible, whether thrones or powers or rulers or authorities; all things have been created through him and for him. ¹⁷ He is before all things, and in him all things hold together. ¹⁸ And he is the head of the body, the church; he is the beginning and the firstborn from among the dead, so that in everything he might have the supremacy. ¹⁹ For God was pleased to have all his

fullness dwell in him, [20] and through him to reconcile to himself all things, whether things on earth or things in heaven, by making peace through his blood, shed on the cross. [Colossians 1:1-5].

As nothing is impossible to God, it is possible for God to take any form and come to earth. Now, is the Lord Jesus Christ God our Creator?

Similarly, the word of God is informative because God teaches us trough His word, when we read the word of God, we learn from God, and we learn about God as God instructs us about His existence, His nature and His creation. God teaches us about Him in many ways including trough nature, His creation [Romans 1:20]; through his Son, our Lord and Savior Jesus Christ: but in these last days he has spoken to us by His Son, whom he appointed heir of all things, and through whom also he made the universe [Hebrews 1:2].

In addition, God speaks to us through his word in the Scriptures as already mentioned and God speaks to us through angels, and through circumstances to mention these. For examples, through Scriptures, the inspired word of God, God teaches us about His nature as the Omniscient, the Omnipotent and the Omnipresence God, the Creator of the universe. God gives prophesies about the Messiah and at the appropriate time, the Messiah came to earth, God came and dwelt among men.

God came and took on flesh and was called Jesus Christ. He came to save His people from sins:

> [21] She will give birth to a son, and you are to give him the name Jesus,[f] because he will save his people from their sins" [Matthew 1:21].

The Lord Jesus was also called Immanuel, God with us [Matthew 1:23] God speaks to us through his inspired word. As already mentioned, through angels, through nature, through circumstances and through numerous uncountable ways.

Concerning nature, God speaks to us through nature as He displays the beauty of His creation. Nature testifies to God's existence as Scriptures instruct us [Romans 1:20]. Nature provides us with powerful evidence to

God's existence because through nature, one realizes the deepness of God's magnitude and the profoundness of His love.

The truth of the cited passage of Scriptures above can be supported by many believers who often seek to find peace by isolating themselves in nature. They isolate themselves and go by the sea near the beach or near the ocean to think and to ponder in quietness to have a clear mind and they are inspired. Who is inspiring them? Poets and writers who spend time by the sea find a peaceful place.

Near the sea or near the ocean is a quiet place to rest and to meditate as most people would agree. When listening carefully to people who seek to retrieve by the ocean to have peace, one realizes that they want to be closer to God and in the nature. When they are alone far from distraction they can sense the presence of God. To think that God can only be found by the sea at the beach or in the mountain or in valleys will be wrong because God is omnipresent, He is everywhere [Psalms 139].

Concerning His nature, God's word teaches that God is Omnipresent and God's creation testifies to God's existence, therefore when a person stands by the sea or near the ocean he or she can sense the Spirit of God powerfully.

Similarly, when one looks in the sky above, during the day or at night, there is a great chance to sense the magnitude of God. Moreover, there is much to learn about God in oral literature and in written literature. The contents of Oral Literature from all societies have shown concerns to discuss the origin of life and have pointed to a Supreme Being who is self existence and Who was not created. For their part the *Baluba* of the Democratic Republic of Congo often refer to *Mikombo,* a self existence character who was not created and who was mysterious. This description fits the passages of [John 1-1-14] that explains that in the beginning was the Word and the Word became Flesh and also the passage of [Colossians 1:15-20].

The Lord Jesus Christ is God, our Creator and He came to earth in the form of Human Being, the baby Jesus was conceived by the power of the holy Spirit:

> ... The angel answered, "The Holy Spirit will come on you, and the power of the Most High will overshadow you. So the holy one to be born will be called[b] the Son of God. [Luke 1: 35].

In addition, the Lord Jesus Christ is called Mighty God and Everlasting Father [Isaiah: 9:6].

The Lord Jesus Christ is God the Almighty: "I am the Alpha and the Omega," says the Lord God, "who is, and who was, and who is to come, the Almighty" [Revelation 1:8].

During His earthly ministry, the LORD taught that there is Only One God, and that He is the Truth, no one goes to the father except through Him, this sentence also teaches us something about the Lord's authority.

Circumstances such as life and death testify to the existence of God and His power to create.

In the presence of death, all creatures recognize God's power and understand that only God has overcome death.

Discussing God's existence and evidence to God's existence constitutes one aspect of the book and as we can see God has provided us with powerful evidence that one cannot deny that God was, God is and God will always be. Along with the first aspect for God's existence is to determine who this God is. Scriptures teach that there is Only One God, Who is powerful, and All knowing and Scriptures assign all the titles they give to God to the Lord Jesus, which leads us to conclude that the LORD Jesus Christ is God our Creator

For examples:

In Scriptures God is described as the Only Savior, and the Lord Jesus Christ is described as the Only Savior.

God is the Only Savior	Jesus is the only Saviour.
"I, even I, am the LORD; and beside me there is no savior." Isaiah 43:11	. . . the Father sent the Son to be the Saviour of the world. 1 John 4:14
To the only wise God our Savior . . . Jude 1:12	. . . our Lord and Saviour Jesus Christ. II Peter 3:18
God our Savior. Titus 2:10	. . . God and our Saviour Jesus Christ. II Peter 1:1
. . . we trust in the living God, who is the Savior. I Timothy 4:10	. . . the Christ, the Saviour of the world. John 4:42
God my Savior. Luke 1:47	. . . the Lord Jesus Christ our Saviour. Titus 1:4 a Saviour, which is Christ the Lord. Luke 2:11
God is the Only Savior	Neither is there salvation in any other (than Jesus): for there is none other name under heaven given among men, whereby we must be saved.
	—Acts 4:12
	. . . salvation . . . is in Christ Jesus with eternal glory.
	—2 Timothy 2:10
	. . . captain of their salvation [Jesus] perfect through sufferings.
	—Heb 2:10
	[Jesus] . . . author of eternal salvation . . .
	—Heb 5:9

There is Only One Who IS Holy, God Himself

Jesus is the Holy One.	*Jesus is the Holy One.*
Acts 2:27 Because thou wilt not leave my soul in hell, neither wilt thou suffer <u>thine Holy One to see corruption.</u>	*Acts 2:27 Because thou wilt not leave my soul in hell, neither wilt thou suffer <u>thine Holy One to see corruption.</u>*
3:13-14 The God of Abraham, and of Isaac, and of Jacob, the God of our fathers, hath <u>glorified his Son Jesus</u>; whom ye delivered up, and denied him in the presence of Pilate, when he was determined to let him go. <u>But ye denied the Holy One</u> and the Just, and desired a murderer to be granted unto you;	*3:13-14 The God of Abraham, and of Isaac, and of Jacob, the God of our fathers, hath <u>glorified his Son Jesus</u>; whom ye delivered up, and denied him in the presence of Pilate, when he was determined to let him go. <u>But ye denied the Holy One</u> and the Just, and desired a murderer to be granted unto you;*
13:34-35 And as concerning that he raised him up from the dead, now no more to return to corruption, he said on this wise, I will give you the sure mercies of David. Wherefore he saith also in another psalm, Thou shalt not suffer <u>thine Holy One to see corruption.</u>	*13:34-35 And as concerning that he raised him up from the dead, now no more to return to corruption, he said on this wise, I will give you the sure mercies of David. Wherefore he saith also in another psalm, Thou shalt not suffer <u>thine Holy One to see corruption.</u>*

Furthermore, God is called Almighty God and the LORD Jesus Christ is called Almighty God. Based on this evidence, we can conclude that there is Only One God as Scriptures teach.

The book of Genesis speaks about God, the Creator, the true God and the Book of John instructs us that God became Man [John 1:-14].

Other evidence to God's existence and to the fact that the LORD Jesus Christ is God our Creator include the fact that our consciousness condemns us when we do wrong or when we do good. God puts on everyone's heart an engine that we call consciousness to tell us when we act wrong. The Lord Jesus Christ is God our Creator because the Lord Jesus Christ knows the thoughts in our hearts [9:4].

God is merciful, and He has shown His mercy by creating men in His own image [Genesis 1:27]; Moreover, the Lord came to earth as a human being to live among men and to save us [Matthew 1:21].

A closer look at the Scripture reveals that, the Lord Jesus Christ lived among us, He accepted worships, He knew peoples' thoughts, He healed the sick, He forgave sins, He decided to go to the cross to suffer and to test death for us, He gave his life to be crucified, He rose himself from the dead, and He conquered death.

Passages from the Old Testament and from the Old Testament teach that there is Only One God and they testify to the truth about Christ's Deity as God our Creator: John 1:1-14; Colossians 1:15-21

- Mark 12:29 Jehovah our God Is One.

Many passages from the Scriptures teach us about creation and point us to the Creator, among those the passage that speak about the Word that was in the beginning, that created everything, and that became Flesh: [1:1-14].

Similarly, Scriptures teach about Christ's supremacy, referring to Him as the Son of God, the firstborn of all creation and in Who dwelt the fullness of God [Colosians 1:15].

Revelation 3 teaches that Christ is the ruler of all creation.

These passages point us to the Creator.

Powerful Scriptures that reveal Christ's Deity and teach that He is our Creator include:

- John 1:2-3—"He [Jesus Christ] was in the beginning with God. *All things were made through Him* and without Him nothing was made."

- John 1:10—"He was in the world, and *the world was made by him*, and the world knew him not."

- 1 Corinthians 8:6—"But to us there is but one God, the Father, of whom are all things, and we in him; and one Lord Jesus Christ, *by whom are all things*, and we by him."

- Colossians 1:16-17—"For by him [Jesus Christ] *were all things created*, . . . all things consist."

- Hebrews 1:2-3—". . . his Son, whom he hath appointed heir of all things, *by whom also he made the worlds*; Who being the brightness of his glory, and the express image of his person, and upholding all things by the word of his power . . . ."

- Hebrews 2:10—"For it became him, for whom are all things, and *by whom are all things* . . . ."

- Hebrews 3:3-4—"For this man [Jesus Christ] was counted worthy of more glory than Moses, inasmuch as *he who hath builded the house* hath more honour than the house. For every house is builded by some man; but he that built all things is God."

Scriptures are the inspired word of God and they teach that God exists and He is our Creator; God created everything that exists, whether spiritual or material: [Acts 17:24]

Also in the Book of Revelation 4:11 we read: "Thou art worthy, O Lord, to receive glory and honor and power: for thou hast created all things, and for thy pleasure they are and were created"

Further, in the same Book, Revelation 10:6: we read: "[Him] that liveth for ever and ever, who created heaven, and the things that therein are, and the earth, and the things that therein are, and the sea, and the things which are therein . . ."

Scriptures teach that the Lord Jesus Christ created everything, this explains the functions of the triune God, the Father, The Son and the Holy Spirit. And also the pluralism nature of God as we read in the Book of Genesis: 1:26: "Let us make man in *our* image, after *our* likeness." Following are some verses of Scripture which teach that Christ is the Creator.

The Lord Jesus Christ is God, our Creator:

Moreover, concerning His existence, Scriptures teach that the Lord Jesus has eternal existence:

- Isaiah 9:6
- John 1:1-3
- John 8:58
- Revelation 1:8
- Revelation 22:13.

From everlasting to everlasting the Lord Jesus lives.

Knowing that there is Only One God, the Great Shepherd in the Old Testament and the New Testament is a blessing: [Ezekiel 34:11-17; 23-29] and [John 10:11]. Many people are aware of God's title as the Great Shepherd of the Old Testament, and they are also aware of the Lord Jesus Christ's claim that He IS the Great "I Am He," and He IS the Shepherd who gives His life for the sheep, but only few believers see the parallelism between several passages from the Old Testament and the New Testament to make analogies of God's title as the Great Shepherd of the Old Testament and the Great Shepherd in the New Testament. Similarly, not many believers believe that God, our Creator is the GREAT I AM of the Old Testament and of the New Testaments as Scriptures teach [Exodus 3:14] [John:8:58]; and as Jehovah, the Creator in the Old Testament and in The New Testament. There is Only One God [Deuteronomy 6:4].

"You are my witnesses," declares the LORD, "and my servant whom I have chosen, so that you may know and believe me and understand that I am he. Before me no god was formed, nor will there be one after me," (Isaiah 43:10).

[29] "The most important one," answered Jesus, "is this: 'Hear, O Israel: The Lord our God, the Lord is one.[e] [30] Love the Lord your God with all your heart and with all your soul and with all your mind and with all your strength.'[f] [31] The second is this: 'Love your neighbor as yourself.'[g] There is no commandment greater than these" [Mark 12:29].

JESUS	IS	GOD, "YAHWEH"
John 1:3, "Through him all things were made; without him nothing was made that has been made."		Job 33:4, "The Spirit of God has made me; the breath of the Almighty gives me life."
Col. 1:16-17, "For by him all things were created: things in heaven and on earth, visible and invisible, whether thrones or powers or rulers or authorities; all things were created by him and for him. He is before all things, and in him all things hold together."	Creator	Isaiah 40:28, "Do you not know? Have you not heard? The LORD is the everlasting God, the Creator of the ends of the earth. He will not grow tired or weary, and his understanding no one can fathom."

The Lord Jesus and the father are One:

- As one with the Father.

- John 10:30 I and *my* Father are one.

- John 12:45

- John 14:7-10]

- John 17:10

God is the Holy One, and The Lord Jesus Christ is the Holy One.

- 1 Samuel 2:2 *There is* none holy as the LORD: for *there is* none beside thee: neither *is there* any rock like our God.

- Acts 3:14 But ye denied the Holy One and the Just, and desired a murderer to be granted unto you;

Conclusion

There is Only One God; faith in God is a gift from God and without faith, it is impossible to please God. We need to believe that God exists and He is our Creator. Few things to remember when discussing the Deity of the Lord Jesus Christ and His Sovereignty include the following, Only God has mercy and compassion beyond imagination to come and die for His People to save them as we read in the Book of Matthew 1:23, Moreover, only God knows peoples' thoughts and the LORD Jesus Christ has proven over and over again that He knows peoples' thoughts and the intentions of the hearts. God looks in the heart while men look at the appearance (I Samuel) and the LORD Jesus Christ has proven numerous times as already mentioned: Knowing their thoughts, Jesus said, "Why do you entertain evil thoughts in your hearts [Matthew 9:4]?"

Resurrection, only God could raise Himself from the dead, no one else could do that [John 10:18]. Based on these simple facts, we can believe that the Lord Jesus Christ is God, Our Creator. These facts and several others provide evidence and testify to Christ's Deity and to His Sovereignty as God, Our Creator. I am He, if ye don't believe you will perish, the Lord says: [John 8:24].

To highlight many powerful arguments, *Christ' Deity: The Deity of the Lord Jesus Christ; Truth, Myth and Challenges* considers passages from various versions including New International Version (NIV Bible) and King James (KJ).

Activities for this Chapter

How do we know God exists and what evidence testifies to God's existence?

_____

_____

_____

_____

Most people who doubt God's existence claim that there is no convincing evidence to testify to God's existence, if you meet a person who does not believe in God, what evidence can you provide them with to help remove their doubts?

_____

_____

_____

_____

3. If you, yourself still have some doubts about God's existence, what kind of evidence would you like to receive in order to believe that God exists?

_____

_____

_____

_____

4) Why do you think many people doubt God's existence and what message can you share with them to help them come closer to God? Can you encourage them to invite the Lord Jesus Christ in their hearts as the Lord ask in the book of Revelation[3:20]?

_____

_____

_____

_____

5. Scriptures teach that there is Only One God [Nehemiah 9:6; 1 Samuel 2:2]. Do you agree with the statements of the following verses?

[Deuteronomy 4:35-39].

[Deuteronomy 32:39].

⁵For there is one God and one mediator between God and mankind, the man Christ Jesus [I Timothy 2:5].

6. The Lord Jesus teaches that there is Only One God [Mark 12:29-22]. What do you think of this passage?

"Jesus answered him, 'The first of all the commandments is: "Hear, O Israel, the LORD our God, the LORD is one. And . . . . sacrifices'" [Mark 12:29-33].

"So Jesus said to him, 'Why do . . . [Mark 10:18; Matthew 19:17].

"How can you believe, who receive honor from one another, and do not seek the honor that comes from the only God?" [John 5:44].

7. What do you think of the passages of John 1:1-14 and the passage of Colossians 1:1-15?

_____

_____

_____

_____

CHAPTER 1

God has Revealed Himself to the World.

For since the creation of the world God's invisible qualities—his eternal power and divine nature—have been clearly seen, being understood from what has been made, so that men are without excuse [Romans 1:20].

How we know God exists.

Scriptures teach that God exists and He is our Creator and that God has chosen to reveal Himself to the world. God reveals Himself in many ways including through nature and through His word, in the Holy Bible. But one powerful way God has revealed Himself is when God became Man and He lived among men. His coming to earth was predicted and at the appropriate time God came to earth and God lived among men[Isaiah 6:9; John 1:14; Matthew 1:21] and [Galatians 4:4]. God also reveals Himself to us through nature, His Creation. Have you ever spent time at the sea and ponder about its hugeness, quietness and tranquility or have you ever imagined standing by some large body of water that spread from side to side and that we call the sea? Have you sometimes seen very huge body of water spreading and being still without moving, that we call a lake; and sometimes even moving and that we call the river? Can you imagine and see the beauty of such body of water? Let me share with you that beauty is the beauty of creation and such beautiful views testify to God's existence.

Moreover, one can imagine being alone in the forest and receiving deep inspiration. Imagine being in a huge forest alone, listening to the singing of the birds and the cries of animals and some little creatures crying for food and praising the Creator. The birds in the forest sing even early in the morning to praise the Creator. Animals and beasts rely on God for food [Job 38:39]. That is powerful evidence to God's existence as the birds sing and praise the Creator, as animals cry to God, wait to be fed by the Hand of the Almighty God who created them and who cares about them. Lions, kings of the forest; leopard, elephants and all the beats, think about these huge and strong animals. Do you think these creatures came to existence by chance and that they were not created by the Almighty God, our Creator and the Creator of the universe? God created everything in the world and all depends on Him for survival.

The beauty of the bodies of water and the beauty of the nature speak volume about the Creator, The Maker of the universe. It cannot be true that seas, rivers, mountains, animals and all the peoples on earth and all creatures in heavens exist by chance without the wisdom or the Mighty Creator who created them. Believing in God is a personal matter. Each individual needs to think about his own existence and ponder about sadness, sicknesses, diseases and death to well appreciate life after death, life in the place where there will be neither grief, pain nor suffering; life in the city of God, where there is neither misery nor poverty and where there will not be the second death because after death, those who believe in Christ will spend eternity with God; they will live forever and will not experience the second death in contrast to those who have rejected Christ and who will experience the second death as Scriptures, the inspired word of God instruct us [Revelation2:11]. Believing in God and accepting Him is a matter of life and death.

Elsewhere, we read also about the second death in the Book of Revelation in the following passages:

> [6] Blessed and holy are those who share in the first resurrection. The second death has no power over them, but they will be priests of God and of Christ and will reign with him for a thousand years [Revelation 20:6].

> [8] But the cowardly, the unbelieving, the vile, the murderers, the sexually immoral, those who practice magic arts, the idolaters and all liars—they will be consigned to the fiery lake of burning sulfur. This is the second death." [Revelation 21:8].

Before we go deeper in discussing rewards for those who believe in God and the punishments and the second death, it is important not to doubt God's existence.

Many questions cross peoples' minds among them the existence of God and the Deity of the Lord Jesus Christ. Most people who refuse to believe in God state that there is no evidence that testifies to God's existence. They put forwards all kinds of arguments to dismiss the truth about God's existence. As I mentioned earlier the most cited argument that is put forward by those who doubt God's existence, is that "there is no evidence that testifies to God's existence." Interestingly enough, this argument which is most presented, "the lack of evidence" to testify to God's existence, is the the argument God has challenged the most with powerful evidence to testify to His existence by showing us such powerful elements as nature, life, death, and childbearing to mention these. The evidence God has presented has been so powerful that the arguments to deny God's existence cannot much the concreteness of the evidence God has presented to testify to His existence.

God reveals Himself to His people in many ways. God reveals Himself through His Word, the Scriptures, and God reveals Himself through Nature, through His Son, through His Audible Voice, through people, through angels and through visions to mention these. There are other numerous ways God reveals Himself to His people. One cannot limit God, and our thoughts are not God's thoughts as we read in Scriptures [Isaiah 55:8]. God cannot be limited.

To understand, we will limit our evidence to the word of God because the word of God is infallible. The Lord Jesus Christ said that Heavens and earth will pass away, not His word [Matthew 24:35].

We can start off our discussion with a powerful statement that God exists and He is our Creator.

How we know God exists and How God teaches us about Himself:

We learn about God when we read His word in the Holy Bible and when we listen to the Scriptures. God has provided His Word in the

Annie Ngana-Mundeke (Ph.D).

Holy Bible to teach us about Himself. Throughout the Scripture, God teaches us about His Existence, about Creation and about numerous other themes including, kinship, family genealogy, the origin of life, about sin, about death, eternal life, about love and forgiveness, about His plan for redemption, the salvation of soul and about the last judgment, about His names, about Who He is, about heaven and hell and several other themes. The Holy Bible speaks about God; it is God's Book, throughout the entire Bible we learn about God.

Moreover, Scriptures teach us that God took the human form and came to earth to live among men. The testimony of God's existence and God's creation are told in written literature, in the Scriptures.

Now, one may argue that there are many people who cannot read or write and how would they learn about God? To answer this question we can also go back to the Scripture as the word of God teaches that heavens proclaimed God's glory:

> [1] The heavens declare the glory of God;
> the skies proclaim the work of his hands.
> [2] Day after day they pour forth speech;
> night after night they reveal knowledge.
> [3] They have no speech, they use no words;
> no sound is heard from them.
> [4] Yet their voice[b] goes out into all the earth,
> their words to the ends of the world.

In the heavens God has pitched a tent for the sun[[Psalms 19:14].

Once again, nature teaches us about God. One does not need to read and write to learn about God and to notice God's creation. God reveals Himself through nature [Romans 1:20]. God also reveals Himself through dreams and visions:

> "And afterward,
> I will pour out my Spirit on all people.
> Your sons and daughters will prophesy,

4

> your old men will dream dreams,
> your young men will see visions [Joel 28].

Moreover, our consciousness teaches us about right and wrong, and reminds us of right and wrong, good and evil every time we do wrong: [20]whenever our hearts condemn us. For God is greater than our hearts, and he knows everything [I John 3:20].

When we do wrong, our consciousness condemns us and it reminds us of right and wrong and testifies to God's existence and to His goodness and indicates to us that we have just acted against God's goodness. Similarly, when our consciousness acts honestly and truly, it testifies to God's existence and to His goodness and gives inner peace in the heart. Now, the word of God teaches us that God exists and He is our Creator [Hebrews 11:5]. When it comes to the existence of God and to evidence to God's existence, most people just know deep in the heart that God exists for they have faith in God and all the evidence around them testifies to God's existence.

Some powerful evidence such as death also speaks loud to God's existence and to His goodness and testifies to his might and power to give life and to take it back.

It was in the Garden of Eden that the LORD stated:

> . . . for dust you are
> and to dust you will return" [Genesis 3:19]

And it was during His ministry on earth that the LORD states:

> No one takes it from me, but I lay it down of my own accord. I have authority to lay it down and authority to take it up again. This command I received from my Father" [John 10:18].

Now, because we close this chapter, I would like to remind the reader of the importance of Oral Literature and its impacts on learning about peoples' cultures, beliefs, geography, history and how it has been a vehicle that has been used by peoples from various societies to teach about God's existence and about His creation.

Many languages have oral literature that include proverbs, folktales, songs, and epics that refer to God, the Creator. For examples, In Deo speramus, ("In God we trust."(Latin); God bless you; In God we trust, (English), Dieu Est Grand, God is Great (French); Mividi Mukulu Udiku. (There is God, God exists indeed. Mvidia Mukulu udi ne Lusa, God is merciful. Gloria A Dios, Glory to God, (Spanish), Mungu akubarikye, God bless you (Swahili); in all the language spoken on this earth there is reference to God, our Creator.

Each language has proverbs that refer to God, the Creator and to His creation. In most languages there are many proverbs and mottos, that refer to the Creator and His creation. For examples, Latin proverbs and mottos refer to the Creator, His creation, His will and His power. Therefore, a motto such as Deo Iuvante Vincamus, God willing we will win; Volente Deo! God willing! There are numerous Latin mottos that refer to God as one can read in dictionaries and classic books: Deus absconditus—A god who is hidden from man; Deus commodo muto consisto quem meus canis sententia existo; God which, in a very ham-fisted way, with generosity, comes close to being; Deus et natua non faciunt frusta—God and nature do not work together in vain; Deus ex machina—A contrived or artificial solution, literally, 'a god from a machine; Deus Misereatur—May God Have Mercy. Deus vobiscum—God be with you; Deus volent—(as) God will; Deus vult!—God wills it! Domine, dirige nos—Lord, direct us; Domino optimo maximo—To the Lord, the best and greatest; Dominus illuminatio mea—The Lord is my light; Dominus providebit—The Lord will provide; Dominus tecum—May the Lord be with you (Singular); Dominus vobiscum—May the Lord be with you (Plural); these mottos are used in most writings by most scholars in reference to God. If God did not exist, why have peoples from all societies and all nations been using oral literature to teach about God and about creation and why do many languages including the classic languages such as Latin and Greg use mottos and says that refer to God?

Scholars who have addressed issues concerning God's existence, God's power and God's creation have demonstrated that there are names of God,

Almighty in most languages that are spoken on earth. But, I personally believe that there are names of God in all languages and that there is no spoken language on earth that has failed to refer to God, our Creator because God exists and He created the heaven and the earth and everything on earth and all men on earth [Acts 17:24]. God empowers human beings with ability to speak and human beings in all societies feel the need to respond to the Creator, A Supreme Being who is powerful and who is above all power, the Almighty God they need to worship. The deepness in the human hearts longs to worship the Creator and to have fellowship with Him.

People in every society share folktales, epics, proverbs, satires, and says that reflect their beliefs and knowledge and that are a part of oral literature. Languages of the words have numerous nouns, verbs, adjectives and adverbs that can be used only to refer to the Almighty God. Folktales and elements of oral literature in all languages use words that mention God, the Creator and God's creations as already mentioned. In his volume, The *Case Against Darwin: Why the Evidence Should Be Examined*, James Perloff one of the writers whose writings defeat the theory of Evolution, makes a powerful statements that folktales in all languages make mention of God, and that if God did not exist and if God's creation was a random action, there would not be so many legends about creation in almost all languages of the world. Although James Perloff was flexible to say that in almost all languages, there are legends about creation, the truth of the matter is that people in all societies seek to worship the Supreme Being who created them and Who is above all. In all languages there is mention of God or of a Supreme Being Who is above all.

In some of my writings, I have discussed the Bantu religious beliefs and the Bantu philosophy that testify to the fact that there are names of God in all Bantu languages. I mean the name of the Almighty God, who has the Power over all; God Who when he decides, no one can change his decisions, just like it is written in the Scriptures when he closes the door, no one can open and when he opens no one can close [Revelation 3:7].

The question is who is the Almighty God? Speaking of the Bantu peoples and their beliefs in the Supreme Being, the Almighty God, the name of God is mentioned in all the Bantu Languages. Therefore. In their philosophical ideologies, and in the lexicons, one finds such names as Nzambe Mpugu, Mividia Mukulu, Mweja, Maweja Mufuiki, Nzambe Monene, Nzambe Na Kuya, Nzambe Mpungu, the Almighty in all Bantu languages including Swahili, Luba, Lingala, Ki-Kongo of the Democratic Republic of the Congo and the Ba Punu of the Republic of Gabon to mention these.

Speaking of this Almighty God, the Baluba of the Democratic Republic of Congo recognize the Supreme Being they call Mikombo Wa Kalowa, Mikombo Nkayehenda Mudifuka, Mikombo is the Almighty God, the Supreme Being who self exists. Interestingly enough is that the name Mikombo points to the Son of God, the LORD Jesus Christ. Growing up, In Kinshasa in the Democratic Republic of Congo, the name Mikombo and its characteristics went beyond my imagination as a child because in the song and in the Folktale, Mikombo is the Self Existence Being Who came to being by Himself. Later, as an adult, I begin to realize that Mikombo character is also described in the Holy Bible when I read such passages as [John 1, 1-14] and [Colossians 1:15—20].

These passages teach us about God, Our Creator Who is above all. After I discovered this connection between *Mikombo* the character in *the Luba* African folktales, I was please, but I still needed some confirmation from other people who know about stories of *Mikombo*. One day, I consulted with one of my elder brothers who confirmed to me that Mikombo character in Luba folktales and *Luba* languages referrers to the LORD Jesus Christ indeed. Mikombo character is not only mentioned in folktales for young children, but also, adults in *Luba* communities are fascinated by Mikombo character, His wisdom and deeds.

As an example of the mention of God and His creation in various languages, I can name here few languages I, the writer of this book speak or simply read or have some kind of knowledge about that testify that God Almighty is mentioned and He has given many names.

More often, it strikes my mind that there is mention of God, the Creator in these languages in some ways even when some people in these societies still believe in other gods, they have the name for the Almighty God, *Mvidia Mukulu*. Well, you may consider them polytheists, but the point that we are trying to get across here is that despite the fact that some people believe in several gods, they have the name of the Almighty God, Who is above all. One can observe these in their languages. Proverbs, mottos, songs, epics and says are few examples of oral literature that make mention of God and His creation and that have been used to recognize God's existence and to praise Him from generations to generations. It has been more than 2000 years since the Lord Jesus Christ lived on earth, was crucified and ascended to heaven, yet classic languages including Latin, and Greek have not dropped God's names from usage, on the contrary, such references as B.C. and A.C are added to the lexicons. If God does not exist and if Christ did not come to earth, why such references to His birth and the use of the expressions "Before Christ" and "After Christ" in World History, one may wonder.

There is evidence to testify to God's existence in oral literature, in written literature and even through nature that everyone can see and in our conscious that we can feel when we do wrong. Our conscious tells us when we do wrong and it condemns us: whenever our hearts condemn us. For God is greater than our hearts, and he knows everything [I John 3:20]

As for nature, everyone can agree that nature testifies to God's existence, and such evidence is obvious that we cannot deny or seek excuses to dismiss the evidence of nature to God's existence or blame God for not revealing Himself.

Scholars of theology inform us of general revelation and special revelation, whatever we wish to trust, there is considerable evidence that testifies to God's existence. Scriptures inform us that God exists and He is our Creator and that without faith it is impossible to please God: [Hebrews 11:6].

The Book of Genesis informs us about God and about creation as we read in chapter 1 and in chapter 2. In the Book of [John 1:1-14] the Scripture point us to the Creator. Truly God exists, He is our Creator and He loves us.

God has numerous attributes and numerous functions. He is the Creator, the Savior, the Healer, the Redeemer, the Shepherd, the Judge, He forgives sins and He has many other titles and functions. God forgives sins, He heals the sick, He is merciful, He is omniscient, He is all powerful, loving and He has numerous functions and attributes as Scriptures teach.

All God's titles and functions are assigned to the Lord Jesus Christ. For example, God is the Shepherd and the Lord Jesus Christ is the shepherd.

God reveals Himself in many ways as I already mentioned, but one of the most powerful way God has revealed Himself to the world is when He came to earth and was called the Lord Jesus Christ, and stated that He is the shepherd [John 10:11]. In both the Old Testament and in the New Testament, we read about the Shepherd who takes care of the sheep [Ezekiel 34:11-17; 23-29] and [John 10:11].

The Lord performed deeds that only God, our Creator could perform these including forgiving sins, healing the sick and raising the death. The Lord is assigned the title of God, our Creator.

God is the Savior and the Lord Jesus Christ is the Savior. God is also the Judge and the Lord Jesus Christ is the Judge. Scriptures describe the Lord Jesus Christ mightily:

- As the Great God and Savior.

  - Hosea 1:7

  - Titus 2:13

- As Jehovah, above all.

  - Psalms 97:9

  - John 3:31

  - Titus 2:13

- As God over all.

  - Psalms 45:6-7

- As Lord of all.

  - Acts 10:36

  - Romans 10:11-13

- As the Eternal God and Creator.

  - Psalms 102:24-27 I said,

  - Hebrews 1:8

  - Hebrews 1:10-12

Conclusion

The Lord Jesus Christ is God, our Creator just as the Scriptures in the Holy Bible teach.

Scriptures present challenges because they are the word of God and the word of God is truth for God does not make mistakes and God does not lie.

Activities for this Chapter.

1. How do we know God exists?

_____

_____

_____

_____

2. What powerful arguments can you provide to help someone or to teach someone about God' existence?

_____

_____

_____

_____

CHAPTER 2

The Deity of the LORD Jesus Christ: Challenges and Responses.

And we know that the Son of God has come and has given us an understanding, that we may know Him who is true; and we are in Him who is true, in His Son Jesus Christ. This is the true God and eternal life [1 John 5:20].KJ

[7] For there are three that bear witness in heaven: the Father, the Word, and the Holy Spirit; and these three are one [1 John 5:7]. KJ

Making a statement that God exists and that He is our Creator is one thing, but recognizing Who God Is, is another issue. Many people agree that there is Only One God, and that God exists. However, many disagree on determining Who God, the Creator of the universe is. Similarly, many scholars believe that there is Only One God, but they have problems to accept the triune God, who is the Father, the Son and the Holy Spirit. Furthermore, many agree that the Lord Jesus Christ is God, He is 100% Man and 100% God, and that in Him dwelled the fullness of Deity [Colossaians1:1-15], But, they refuse to believe that the Lord Jesus Christ is God the Creator according to the Scriptures. As we read in the Holy Bible, Scriptures teach that In Christ, dwells the Fullness of Deity [Colossaians1:1-15] and that the Word Became Flesh [John 1:1-14].

God is the Shepherd and the Lord Jesus is the Shepherd

God reveals Himself in many ways as I already mentioned, but one of the most powerful way God has revealed Himself to the world is when He came to earth and was called the Lord Jesus Christ. Scriptures teach that God is the Shepherd. In both the Old Testament and in the New Testament, we read about the Shepherd who takes care of the sheep:

- God is described as Jehovah the Shepherd.

Isaiah 40, He shall feed his flock like a shepherd: he shall gather the lambs with his arm, and carry *them* in his bosom, *and* shall gently lead those that are with young.

Hebrews 13:20, Now the God of peace, that brought again from the dead our Lord Jesus, that great shepherd of the sheep, through the blood of the everlasting covenant,

[Ezekiel 34: 11—17; 23-29]

The LORD Will Be Israel's Shepherd [Ezekiel chapter 34. Later, in the Book of John 10:11, the Lord Jesus Christ declared that he is the good shepherd:

> [11] "I am the good shepherd. The good shepherd lays down his life for the sheep [John 10:11].

- The Lord Jesus is described as Jehovah, for whose glory all things were created.

Proverbs 16:4

Colossians 1:16

- The Lord Jesus Christ is also described as Jehovah's Fellow and Who is Equal to God.

Zechariah 13:7

Philippians 2:6. Who, being in the form of God, thought it not robbery to be equal with God:

- The Lord is also described as Jehovah God, for whose glory all things in heavens and all things on earth were created.

Proverbs 16:4

Colossians 1:16

God is Eternal and the Lord Jesus Christ is Eternal:

- As Eternal.

  Isaiah 9:6.

  Micah 5:2.

  John 1:1 In the beginning was the Word, and the Word was with God, and the Word was God.

  Colossians 1:17 And he is before all things, and by him all things consist.

  Hebrews 1:8-10:

  Revelation 1:8 I am Alpha and Omega, the beginning and the ending, saith the Lord, which is, and which was, and which is to come, the Almighty.

Moreover, the LORD Himself teaches that He and His Father are ONE:

"… I and the Father are one." [John 10:30].

In the Book of John [1:1-14], we read that the Word became Flesh and in the Book of Colossians [1:1-15], we read about Who created everything [John 1-1-14].

Several scholars have written about the Deity of the LORD Jesus Christ to show the truth of the Scriptures. For his part reverend Matt has provided a table with juxtaposed passages from the Scriptures that testify to the Lord Jesus Christ's Deity:

If you don't believe that I am he, you will perish.

There is a list of miracles and events that the Lord Jesus Christ has performed and that no one else can do, but God Himself. Those events include:

- Forgiving sins: [Mark 2: 9—12].

- Knowing peoples' thoughts: [Matthew 9:4; Matthew 12:25; Luke 9:47;]

- Raising people from death: [Matthew 9:18-26].

- Producing miracles such as multiplying bread and fish to feed thousands peoples [Matthew 14:13-21]; Mark 6:30]

- Walking on water: [Matthew 14:22-33; Mark 6:45-52; and John 6:16-21]

- Accepting worshiped: [Matthew 9:18; Hebrews 1:6; and [20:28].

- From His birth [Mt. 2:1-2) to His ascension [Luke 24:51-52].

- Accepting to be prayed to: [Acts 7:59]

- Possessing absolute Authority [John 14:13].

The Lord Jesus Christ's Claim:

The best way to know a person is to note what the person says he or she is. The Lord Jesus Christ Himself teaches that He is God. Many passages in the Scriptures give insights about what the Lord Jesus Christ said He is. Basically, the Lord Jesus Christ indicated that He is God, our Creator: "I and the Father are one" [John 10:30].

> I told you that you would die in your sins; if you do not believe that I am the one I claim to be,[a] you will indeed die in your sins" [John 8:24].

Elsewhere, God elaborates with Scriptures to show that the LORD is God. They explain how the Lord Jesus Christ is Jehovah. An example worth to me mentioned here is the juxtaposed table of Biblical verses by reverend Matt Slick, who showed that the LORD Jesus Christ is God, the Creator. Just as the LORD said, "the Father and I are ONE."

A glance at this table reveals that there is Only One God. Just as the LORD Jesus said in His preaching:

1.　　*Table by Matt Slick:*

- Jesus is God
- *by Matt Slick*
- "You are my witnesses," declares the LORD, "and my servant whom I have chosen, so that you may know and believe me and understand that I am he. Before me no god was formed, nor will there be one after me," (Isaiah 43:10).

JESUS	IS	GOD, "YAHWEH"
John 1:3, "Through him all things were made; without him nothing was made that has been made."		Job 33:4, "The Spirit of God has made me; the breath of the Almighty gives me life."
Col. 1:16-17, "For by him all things were created: things in heaven and on earth, visible and invisible, whether thrones or powers or rulers or authorities; all things were created by him and for him. He is before all things, and in him all things hold together."	Creator	Isaiah 40:28, "Do you not know? Have you not heard? The LORD is the everlasting God, the Creator of the ends of the earth. He will not grow tired or weary, and his understanding no one can fathom."

Rev. 1:17, "When I saw him, I fell at his feet as though dead. Then he placed his right hand on me and said: 'Do not be afraid. I am the First and the Last.'"

Rev. 2:8, "To the angel of the church in Smyrna write: These are the words of him who is the First and the Last, who died and came to life again."

Rev. 22:13, "I am the Alpha and the Omega, the First and the Last, the Beginning and the End."

First and Last

Isaiah 41:4, "Who has done this and carried it through, calling forth the generations from the beginning? I, the LORD—with the first of them and with the last—I am he."

Isaiah 44:6, "This is what the LORD says—Israel's King and Redeemer, the LORD Almighty: I am the first and I am the last; apart from me there is no God."

Isaiah 48:12, "Listen to me, O Jacob, Israel, whom I have called: I am he; I am the first and I am the last."

John 8:24, "Therefore I said to you that you will die in your sins; for if you do not believe that I am He, you will die in your sins." (NKJV)

John 8:58, "I tell you the truth," Jesus answered, "before Abraham was born, I am!" See Exodus 3:14

John 13:19, "I am telling you now before it happens, so that when it does happen you will believe that I am He."

I AM "ego eimi"

Exodus 3:14, "God said to Moses, "I AM WHO I AM. This is what you are to say to the Israelites: 'I AM has sent me to you.'"

Isaiah 43:10, "You are my witnesses," declares the LORD, "and my servant whom I have chosen, so that you may know and believe me and understand that I am he. Before me no god was formed, nor will there be one after me."

See also Deut. 32:39

2 Tim. 4:1, "In the presence of God and of Christ Jesus, who will judge the living and the dead, and in view of his appearing and his kingdom, I give you this charge . . ."

2 Cor. 5:10, "For we must all appear before the judgment seat of Christ, that each one may receive what is due him for the things done while in the body, whether good or bad."

Judge

Joel 3:12, "Let the nations be roused; let them advance into the Valley of Jehoshaphat, for there I will sit to judge all the nations on every side."

Rom. 14:10, "You, then, why do you judge your brother? Or why do you look down on your brother? For we will all stand before God's judgment seat."

Matt. 2:2, " . . . Where is the one who has been born king of the Jews? We saw his star in the east and have come to worship him."

Luke 23:3, "So Pilate asked Jesus, "Are you the king of the Jews?" "Yes, it is as you say," Jesus replied."

See also John 19:21

King

Jer. 10:10, "But the LORD is the true God; he is the living God, the eternal King. When he is angry, the earth trembles; the nations cannot endure his wrath."

Isaiah 44:6-8, "This is what the LORD says—Israel's King and Redeemer, the LORD Almighty: I am the first and I am the last; apart from me there is no God."

See also Psalm 47

John 8:12,"When Jesus spoke again to the people, he said, "I am the light of the world. Whoever follows me will never walk in darkness, but will have the light of life."

Luke 2:32, "a light for revelation to the Gentiles and for glory to your people Israel."

See also John 1:7-9
1 Cor. 10:4, " . . . for they drank from the spiritual rock that accompanied them, and that rock was Christ."

See also 1 Pet. 2:4-8.

John 4:42, "They said to the woman, 'We no longer believe just because of what you said; now we have heard for ourselves, and we know that this man really is the Savior of the world.'"

1 John 4:14, "And we have seen and testify that the Father has sent his Son to be the Savior of the world."

Light

Rock

Savior

Psalm 27:1, "The LORD is my light and my salvation—whom shall I fear?"

Isaiah 60:20,"our sun will never set again, and your moon will wane no more; the LORD will be your everlasting light, and your days of sorrow will end."

1 John 1:5, "God is light; in him there is no darkness at all."

Deut. 32:4, "He is the Rock, his works are perfect, and all his ways are just. A faithful God who does no wrong, upright and just is he."

See also 2 Sam. 22:32 and Isaiah 17:10.

Isaiah 43:3, "For I am the LORD, your God, the Holy One of Israel, your Savior"

Isaiah 45:21, " . . . And there is no God apart from me, a righteous God and a Savior; there is none but me."

	Shepherd	
John 10:11, "I am the good shepherd. The good shepherd lays down his life for the sheep."		Psalm 23:1, "The LORD is my shepherd, I shall not be in want."
Heb. 13:20, "May the God of peace, who through the blood of the eternal covenant brought back from the dead our Lord Jesus, that great Shepherd of the sheep,"		Isaiah 40:11, "He tends his flock like a shepherd: He gathers the lambs in his arms and carries them close to his heart; he gently leads those that have young."

See also John 10:14,16; 1 Pet. 2:25

- Unless otherwise noted, all quotations are from the NASB.

The Lord Jesus Christ is 100% God and 100 % Man. He was conceived by the Power of the Holy Spirit and He took on the Human Flesh. In Him lived the full Deity.

There are few challenges surrounding Christ's Deity and some people question how Christ could be God when he is referred to in the Scriptures as the Son of Man and as He called Himself the Son of Man and He often speaks of His father and He constantly prayed to the Father. Prior to getting further with the discussion, it is important to note that the title "Son God." has the same meaning of God, God's Son is God. The Son of Man has the nature of God. It is important to recall that one of the reasons, the Pharisees had problems with Christ during His earthly ministry was that they wanted to kill Him because He said that He is the Son of Man.

It is true that many verses refer to the LORD Jesus as the Son of God. For Examples:

Again the high priest asked him, "Are you the Messiah, the Son of the Blessed One?"

[62] "I am," said Jesus. "And you will see the Son of Man sitting at the right hand of the Mighty One and coming on the clouds of heaven [Mark 14:61 b- 62].

[66] At daybreak the council of the elders of the people, both the chief priests and the teachers of the law, met together, and Jesus was led before them. [67] "If you are the Messiah," they said, "tell us."

Jesus answered, "If I tell you, you will not believe me, [68] and if I asked you, you would not answer. [69] But from now on, the Son of Man will be seated at the right hand of the mighty God."

[70] They all asked, "Are you then the Son of God?"

He replied, "You say that I am."

[71] Then they said, "Why do we need any more testimony? We have heard it from his own lips" [Luke 22:66-70].

And yes, the Lord Jesus Christ calls Himself the Son of Man. As Man, He worshiped the father and as God, He was worshiped. As A Man the Lord grew in wisdom, as God He knew everything.

The Lord Jesus Christ is the most important historical character who has ever lived since he is the savior, God in human flesh. The Lord Jesus Christ is not half God and half man, but He is fully divine on one hand, and fully man on the other hand. In other words, Jesus has two distinct natures: "divine nature and human nature."

As divine, He creates and as Human He went to the cross to die for our sin.

The Lord Jesus is the Word who was God and Who was with God and Who became Flesh to save His people from sin: [John 1:1, 14]. This means that Jesus is both human and divine nature, God and man. The divine nature was not changed when the Word became flesh (John 1:1,14). Instead, the

Word was joined with humanity (Col. 2:9). Jesus' divine nature did not change. Similarly the Lord Jesus is not merely a man who neither "had God within Him" nor is he a man who "manifested the God principle." He is God in flesh, He is the Son of God, He is the second person of the trinity, as we read in Scriptures, the inspired word of God. "The Son is the radiance of God's glory and the exact representation of his being, sustaining all things by his powerful word," (Heb. 1:3). Jesus' two natures are not "mixed together, they are separate yet act as a unit in the one person of Jesus. What some scholars refer to as the triune God and other still refer to a Hypostatic Union.

As God the Creator, the Lord Jesus accepted to be worshipped, but as A Man the Lord worshipped the Father.

Once again, in His works, reverend Matt Slick provides a juxtaposition of verses from selected passages of the Bible to illustrate the nature of the Lord Jesus Christ as God and as Man simultaneously and explains that the LORD Jesus Christ is not half man, half God, but He is fully divine and fully man. The Lord has two distinct natures, divine and human, He is the Word that became Flesh as the passage of John 1-1-14 teaches us; He is God and Man. When the Lord Jesus Became Man, He did not change as it is written, "Jesus Christ is the Same yesterday, today and forever [Hebrews 8:13]. The LORD Jesus Christ is God in flesh, the visible image of God [Col. 2:9], in Him dwells the fullness of Deity [Heb. 1:3].

A table of the juxtaposed passages from the Old Testament and passages from the New Testament by Matt Slick can help us to compare and realize that there is Only One God as the table of the juxtaposed verses from Scriptures by Reverend Matt Slick illustrates

It is true that the Deity of the Lord Jesus is challenging, however, the Lord, Himself helps us to understand who He is. We need the Lord's help to know who He is. Unless the Lord reveals Himself to us, none of us could believe that the Lord Jesus Christ is God, our Creator. A glance at the Scriptures reveals that during His earthly ministry, the LORD asked His disciples the crucial question of life and death, a question of faith and revelation: "Who do you say I am? When Peter answered correctly, the Lord stated that the Holy Spirit revealed the answer to Peter:

Peter Declares That Jesus Is the Messiah

[13] When Jesus came . . .

[20] Then he ordered his disciples not to tell anyone that he was the Messiah [Matthew 16:13-20].

Elsewhere in the Scriptures, Paul teaches that no one can say Jesus is Lord unless by the power of Holy Spirit. God reveals Himself. Only by God's grace can one believe that the Lord Jesus Christ is Who He says He is [John 8:24]; God, our Creator.

The Deity of the LORD Jesus Christ is challenged with good reason. First of all it takes His grace and mercy to understand that there is Only One God and He is God the Creator. Unless the LORD opens one's eyes and clarifies the mind to allow the person to see through the lenses of the Holy Spirit there is no way one can accept or believe that Jesus Christ is God the Creator. Speaking for myself, as a writer of this book, when I was young I was baptized as a baby. I did not understand anything about Deity. As I grew up I started believing in the three Gods working as One God without understanding of the Triune God. As a teenager, especially when I reached some maturity, when I was in my twenties, I was blessed to believe in One God, the LORD Jesus Christ playing three functions as the Father, the Son, and the Holy Spirit, I believed and I shared this powerful message with my family members, including my brother Andre Tshibamba Mundeke who was thankful that I shared special information with him and I also shared with others, but never got a chance to write about the Deity of the LORD Jesus Christ. Now, as a mature woman the LORD showed me amazing grace to understand more about His Deity and to write about it.

As I mentioned in this book, God teaches us about His Deity and about Creation in many ways. the most cited argument that is put forward is that there is no evidence to testify to God's existence. However God has provided powerful evidence through nature, and through His Son. When He came on earth and took on Flesh and was called the Lord Jesus Christ and was called Immanuel which means God with us; Matthew 1:23

He came to save His people from sins [Matthew 1:21].

God has provided more than enough evidence, each individual can be moved by one or the other.

Some people do not even have a problem believing that the LORD Jesus Christ is God the Creator. My sister Tony explained to me that she believes since she was in elementary school.

The Deity of the LORD Jesus Christ is an issue of death and life because the Lord is the way, the truth and life [John 14:6]. The Lord said that because He lives, we will also live: ¹⁹ Before long, the world will not see me anymore, but you will see me. Because I live, you will also live [John 14:19].

Thomas called Him, "Lord, we don't know where you are going, so how can we know the way?"

The Lord Jesus Christ gives eternal life [John 6:54-58]:

Also, the Lord Jesus Christ gives Eternal Life: [John 6:54]

His birth was predicted and He accomplished mighty events as described by prophecies. For examples: [Isaiah 6:9]; [Isaiah 7:14]; and [Daniel 7:13-14].

The New Testament: Christ's Coming Recorded:

The Lord Jesus fulfilled the Old testament prophecies.

The Bible teaches that the Lord Jesus Christ is God. For example, prophesies about the divine Messiah predicted in the Old testament teach us that the Lord Jesus Christ is God, our Creator, for examples:

- His birth was predicted: [Isaiah 7:14] *"Therefore the Lord himself will give you a sign: The virgin will be with child and will give birth to a son, and will call him Immanuel."*

- The name Immanuel" literally means: "God with us, as we read in the book of Matthew 1:23; the Lord Jesus Christ was "God with us human beings."

25

- The was born as a human, the Son of God, 100% Human and 100% God, but He has the highest nature as we read in the book of Isaiah: *"For to us a child is born, to us a son is given, and the government will be on his shoulders. And He will be called Wonderful Counselor, Mighty God, Everlasting Father, Prince of Peace"* [Isaiah 9:6].

- The prophet Daniel predicted the coming of the Messiah,

- "There before me was one like a son of man, coming with the clouds of heaven . . . He was given authority, glory and sovereign power; all peoples, nations and men of every language worshiped him. His dominion is an everlasting dominion that will not pass away, and his kingdom is one that will never be destroyed" [Daniel 7:13-14]

"Son of Man" was the primary title Jesus used for Himself—and this passage shows that this was a clear and strong claim of Deity. For example, in the Book of Mark 14: 62, we read: "I am," said Jesus. "And you will see the Son of Man sitting at the right hand of the Mighty One and coming on the clouds of heaven." This statement by our Lord made His listeners angry, they rejected His teaching and decided to kill Him.

During His earthly ministry, the Lord Jesus Christ fulfilled prophesies and He performed miracles and accomplished the deeds that Only God, our Creator could do including healing the sick, forgiving sins and raising the dead.

Moreover, the Lord Jesus Christy was worshiped. First by the Magi and later by His disciples:

Worship by the Magi: [Matthew 2:11]

Worship by His disciples: [Matthew 14:32-33].

Christ's Claim about His Deity. More important to consider in the discussions about Christ's Deity is the Lord's own claims about Himself. The following passages inform us about Christ's claims about His Deity:

"'I tell you the truth,' Jesus answered, 'before Abraham was born, I am!' At this, they picked up stones to stone him, but Jesus hid himself, slipping away from the temple grounds" [John 8:58-59].

Many things can be learned from this passage, first we learn that the Lord Jesus Christ pre-existed His human birth and was actually alive and present (as God) before Abraham; secondly, we lean that that His title was "I am"—which was the same title used for Jehovah God in the Old Testament, more precisely in the book of Exodus [Exodus 3:14]

These powerful statements upset the audience and pushed them to seek to find reasons to execute Him.

- Moreover, in the Book of John, Our Lord stated:

"[30] I and the Father are one."

[31] Again his Jewish opponents picked up stones to stone him, [32] but Jesus said to them, "I have shown you many good works from the Father. For which of these do you stone me?"

[33] "We are not stoning you for any good work," they replied, "but for blasphemy, because you, a mere man, claim to be God." [John 10:30-33]

This is a very clear statement when our Lord claimed His Deity and did not worry about His listeners' reactions, He knew that most of them did not believe Him and they wanted to murder Him. In the end, the Lord was falsely accused, and He gave His Precious Life and shared His Precious Blood to redeem us. Later, after resurrection, many realized that the Lord was really who He said He was. For example, Thomas realized Christ's Deity and stated: "My LORD and My GOD."

"Then He said to Thomas, 'Put your finger here; see my hands. Reach out your hand and put it into my side. Stop doubting and believe.' Thomas said to him, 'My Lord and my God!' Then Jesus told him, 'Because you have seen me, you have believed; blessed are those who have not seen and yet have believed'" [John 20:27-29]. The Lord accepted Thomas's worship because He is Our Creator.

The Lord Jesus Christ accepted worship also prior to His ascended:

> "Then the eleven disciples went to Galilee, to the mountain where Jesus had told them to go. When they saw him, they worshiped him; but some doubted" [Matthew 28:16-17].

> The Lord was worshipped since His birth during His ministry, after resurrection, at His ascension and even today. We pray to Him. He forgives sins, He heals the sick and gives life

Other passages that teach Christ's Deity can be found in the Book of Colossians, the book of Titus, the Book of Hebrews, and in the Book of Revelation:

Colossians 1: 15

"He is the image of the invisible God, the firstborn over all creation. For by him all things were created: things in heaven and on earth, visible and invisible, whether thrones or powers or rulers or authorities; all things were created by him and for him . . . . For in Christ all the fullness of the Deity lives in bodily form [Colossians 1:15-16; 2:9].

Titus 2:13-14. "our great God and Savior, Jesus Christ, who gave himself for us to redeem us.

The Lord Jesus Christ will be worshipped by every creature.

Philippians: Every knee shall bow: [9]

> Therefore God exalted him to the highest place
>   and gave him the name that is above every name,
> [10] that at the name of Jesus every knee should bow,
>   in heaven and on earth and under the earth,

¹¹ and every tongue acknowledge that Jesus Christ is Lord,
to the glory of God the Father.

There are other passages that teach the authority of the LORD Jesus Christ:

Then I heard every creature in heaven and on earth and under the earth and on the sea, and all that is in them, singing: 'To him who sits on the throne and to the Lamb be praise and honor and glory and power, for ever and ever!' The four living creatures said, 'Amen,' and the elders fell down and worshiped." [Revelation 5:13-14].

The Lord Jesus Christ is the Lamb of God who takes away the sins of the world:[John 1:29]. Only God's Blood can cleanse us. He came to the world to redeem us He came to earth to redeem us. He is the Almighty God our Creator:

I am Alpha and Omega, the beginning and the ending, saith the Lord, which is, and which was, and which is to come, the Almighty [Revelation 1:8];

And when Abram was ninety years old and nine, the LORD appeared to Abram, and said unto him, I am the Almighty God; walk before me, and be thou perfect [Genesis 17:1].

Recognizing the Lord's Deity and accepting that He is God our Creator is rewarding for the Lord says that

He gives life:

> My sheep listen to my voice; I know them, and they follow me.
> ²⁸ I give them eternal life, and they shall never perish; no one will
> snatch them out of my hand [John 10 27-28].

He gives eternal life:

> Do not work for food that spoils, but for food that endures to
> eternal life, which the Son of Man will give you. For on him God
> the Father has placed his seal of approval" [John 6:27].

He is the Light of the world: "I am the light of the world. Whoever follows me will never walk in darkness, but will have the light of life [John 8:12].

The worship subject is a significant evidence to considered in the discussions about Christ's Deity because Scriptures, the inspired word of God teach that only God is to be worshipped, and a closer examination of Scriptures reveals that the Lord Jesus Christ was worshipped as we read in the following passages:

- Matthew [2:1-2].

- Matthew [2:10-11].

   After reading these passages, it is logical to conclude that the Lord Jesus Christ is God, our Creator.

Conclusion

The LORD Jesus Christ is God our Creator as Scriptures teach us. His birth was predicted and He performed miracles that Only God could perform such as raising people from death. Only the Lord Jesus has raised people from the dead. Who else has the power to give his life and take it again but God?

- The Lord Jesus Christ never sinned: [46] Can any of you prove me guilty of sin? [John 8:46]

Activities for this Chapter.

What do Scriptures teach about the Lord Jesus Christ?

_____

_____

_____

_____

Who do you say the LORD Jesus Christ Is?

_____

_____

_____

_____

CHAPTER 3

There is Only One God

'You are My witnesses,' says the LORD, 'And My servant whom I have chosen, that you may know and believe Me, and understand that I am He. Before Me there was no God formed, nor shall there be after Me. I, even I, am the LORD, and besides Me there is no savior" [Isaiah 43:10-11].

God has given us Scriptures, His divine word to teach us about His creation, about His will and about Himself. The word of God teaches that there is only One God; we read this in the Old Testament and in the New Testament. We need to rely on God to help us understand His word and to believe in Him. We need to believe in Scriptures because they are the breathed word of God [2 Timothy 3: 16]. Scriptures teach truth for the word of God is truth [John 17:17]. Scriptures teach that without faith it is impossible to please God and that by faith we believe that the world was formed by God:

> And without faith it is impossible to please God, because anyone who comes to him must believe that he exists and that he rewards those who earnestly seek him [Hebrews 11:6].

Scriptures are the word of God and the Word of God is the Lord Jesus Christ Who Is truth truth and life as He said: Jesus answered, "I am the way and the truth and the life. No one comes to the Father except through me[John 14:6]. as He said [John 14:6] When we read Scriptures, the Lord God speaks to us. The LORD says that He and the Father are One. The Lord Jesus Christ teaches that there is Only One God and that He and the Father are One: "I and the Father are one" [John 10:30].

To well address this challenging issue about the Only One God, we need to rely on the Scriptures in the Holy Bible. While examining Scriptures, we will consider various factors including: 1) The Truth and the authority of the Scriptures, 2) The testimonies by the prophets, the apostles, the disciples, and by various writers who wrote various Books in the Holy Bible. 3) The teachings and the discussions of our Lord and Savior Jesus Christ and His views on the Only One True God and 4) The premises of logic.

1) The Truth and the Authority of the Scriptures.

Scriptures teach us that there is Only One God as we read in various passages in the Holy Bible.

In the passages from the Old Testament, we read:

- "Know therefore this day, and consider it in your heart, that the LORD Himself is God in heaven above, and on the earth beneath: there is no other." (Deuteronomy 4:39 NKJV)
- "I am the LORD, and there is no other, there is no God beside Me." (Isaiah 45:5)
- "Have we not all one Father? Has not one God created us?" (Malachi 2:10)
- "Hear, O Israel: the Lord our God, the LORD is one! You shall love the LORD your God with all your heart, with all your soul, and with all your strength." (Deuteronomy 6:4,5)

In the passages from the New Testament, we read:

- "It is written, 'You shall worship the LORD your God, and Him only you shall serve.'" (Matthew 4:10)
- "There is one God; and there is no other but He." (Mark 12:32)
- "You believe that there is one God; you do well." (James 2:19)
- "Now a mediator does not mediate for one only, but God is one." (Galatians 3:20)
- "For there is one God, and one Mediator between God and men." (1 Timothy 2:5)

2) The Testimonies by the Prophets, the Apostles, the Disciples, and by various Writers who wrote various Books in the Holy Bible.

The truth of the fact that there IS Only One God is accepted by many including prophets and disciples.

> "And God spoke all these words, saying: 'I am the LORD your God, who brought you out of the land of Egypt, out of the house of bondage. You shall have no other gods before Me." (Exodus 20:1-3).

> And we know that the Son of God has come and has given us an understanding, that we may know Him who is true; and we are in Him who is true, in His Son Jesus Christ. This is the true God and eternal life [1 John 5:20].KJ

> [7] For there are three that bear witness in heaven: the Father, the Word, and the Holy Spirit; and these three are one [1 John 5:7]. KJ

In Addition, in the Book of Isaiah, we read that there is Only One God.

Many passages in the Scriptures and many servants of God have indicated to us in various circumstances that there is Only ONE GOD. For examples in the Book of Deuteronomy we read:

"To you it was shown, that you might know that the LORD Himself is God; there is none other besides Him . . . . Therefore know this day, and consider it in your heart, that the LORD Himself is God in heaven above and on the earth beneath; there is no other." (Deuteronomy 4:35-39).

"'Now see that I, even I, am He, and there is no God besides Me; I kill and I make alive; I wound and I heal; nor is there any who can deliver from My hand." (Deuteronomy 32:39).

In the book of Joshua we read:

"And as soon as we heard these things, our hearts melted; neither did there remain any more courage in anyone because of you, for the LORD your God, He is God in heaven above and on earth beneath." (Joshua 2:11).

"The Reubenites and the Gadites called the altar Witness; 'For,' said they, 'it is a witness between us that the LORD is God.'" (Joshua 22:34).

And in the Book of Judges were read:

> "But Joash said to all who were arrayed against him, 'Will you contend for Baal? Or will you defend his cause? Whoever contends for him shall be put to death by morning. If he is a god, let him contend for himself, because his altar has been pulled down" [Judges 6:31].

In the Book of I Samuel Hannah, the servant of God Most High states:

> "No one is holy like the LORD, for there is none besides You, nor is there any rock like our God." (1 Samuel 2:2).

As for David He prayed:

> "Therefore You are great, O Lord GOD. For there is none like You, nor is there any God besides You, according to all that we have heard with our ears." (2 Samuel 7:22).

> "O LORD, there is none like You, nor is there any God besides You, according to all that we have heard with our ears." (1 Chronicles 17:20).

> "For who is God, except the LORD? And who is a rock, except our God?" (Psalm 18:31, 2 Samuel 22:32).

> "For You are great, and do wondrous things; You alone are God." (Psalm 86:10).

And for His part, Solomon said to God Most High:

> "And may these words of mine, with which I have made supplication before the LORD, be near the LORD our God day and night, that He may maintain the cause of His servant and the cause of His people Israel, as each day may require, that all the

peoples of the earth may know that the LORD is God; there is no other." [1 Kings 8:59-60].

In the Book of First Kings, Elijah the prophet recognized the fact that there is Only One God:

"Now when all the people saw it, they fell on their faces; and they said, 'The LORD, He is God! The LORD, He is God!'" (1 Kings 18:39).

And Elisha, Elijah's servant in the book of 2 kings said:

"And he returned to the man of God, he and all his aides, and came and stood before him; and he said, 'Indeed, now I know that there is no God in all the earth, except in Israel; now therefore, please take a gift from your servant.'" (2 Kings 5:15).

In the Book of Hezekiah, we read:

"Then Hezekiah prayed before the LORD, and said: 'O LORD God of Israel, the One who dwells between the cherubim, You are God, You alone, of all the kingdoms of the earth. You have made heaven and earth. Incline Your ear, O LORD, and hear; open Your eyes, O LORD, and see; and hear the words of Sennacherib, which he has sent to reproach the living God. Truly, LORD, the kings of Assyria have laid waste the nations and their lands, and have cast their gods into the fire; for they were not gods, but the work of men's hands—wood and stone. Therefore they destroyed them. Now therefore, O LORD our God, I pray, save us from his hand, that all the kingdoms of the earth may know that You are the LORD God, You alone.'" (2 Kings 19:15-19).

"O LORD of hosts, God of Israel, the One who dwells between the cherubim, You are God, You alone, of all the kingdoms of the earth. You have made heaven and earth." (Isaiah 37:16).

The prophet Isaiah instructs us more about the Only One God:

> "'You are My witnesses,' says the LORD, 'And My servant whom I have chosen, that you may know and believe Me, and understand that I am He. Before Me there was no God formed, nor shall there be after Me. I, even I, am the LORD, and besides Me there is no savior." (Isaiah 43:10-11).

> "Thus says the LORD, the King of Israel, and his Redeemer, the LORD of hosts: 'I am the First and I am the Last; besides Me there is no God. And who can proclaim as I do? Then let him declare it and set it in order for Me, since I appointed the ancient people. And the things that are coming and shall come, let them show these to them. Do not fear, nor be afraid; have I not told you from that time, and declared it? You are My witnesses. Is there a God besides Me? Indeed there is no other Rock; I know not one.'" (Isaiah 44:6-8).

"I am the LORD, and there is no other; there is no God besides Me. I will gird you, though you have not known Me, that they may know from the rising of the sun to its setting that there is none besides Me. I am the LORD, and there is no other; I form the light and create darkness, I make peace and create calamity; I, the LORD, do all these things.'" (Isaiah 45:5-7).

"Thus says the LORD: 'The labor of Egypt and merchandise of Cush and of the Sabeans, men of stature, shall come over to you, and they shall be yours; they shall walk behind you, they shall come over in chains; and they shall bow down to you. They will make supplication to you, saying, "Surely God is in you, and there is no other; th*ere is no other God*" [Isaiah 45:14].

"'Tell and bring forth your case; Yes, let them take counsel together. Who has declared this from ancient time? Who has told it from that time? Have not I, the LORD? And there is no other God besides Me, a just God and a Savior; there is none besides Me. Look to Me, and be saved, all you ends of the earth! For I am God, and there is no other.'" (Isaiah 45:21-22).

"Remember the former things of old, for I am God, and there is no other; I am God, and there is none like Me . . ." (Isaiah 46:9).

In the Book of Hosea, we read:

> "Yet I am the LORD your God ever since the land of Egypt, and you shall know no God but Me; for there is no savior besides Me." (Hosea 13:4).

In the Book of Jeremiah, we read:

> "Inasmuch as there is none like You, O LORD (You are great, and Your name is great in might), who would not fear You, O King of the nations? . . . But the LORD is the true God; He is the living God and the everlasting King . . . . hosts is His name" Jeremiah 10:6-16].

In the Book of Joel, we read:

"Then you shall know that I am in the midst of Israel: I am the LORD your God and there is no other. My people shall never be put to shame" [Joel 2:27].

Finally we need to hear from the LORD Himself during His earthly ministry the Lord teaches that there is Only One God as we read in the following passages:

- "Jesus answered him, 'The first of all the commandments is: "Hear, O Israel, the LORD our God, the LORD is one. And you shall love the LORD your God with all your heart, with all your soul, with all your mind, and with all your strength." This is the first commandment. (Mark 12:29-33).
- "So Jesus said to him, 'Why do you call Me good? No one is good but One, that is, God." (Mark 10:18; Matthew 19:17).
- "How can you believe, who receive honor from one another, and do not seek the honor that comes from the only God?" (John 5:44).

In the New Testament, in the book of James we read:

"You believe that there is one God. You do well. Even the demons believe—and tremble!" (James 2:19).

For His part the apostle Paul writes:

> "Or is He the God of the Jews only? Is He not also the God of the Gentiles?" [Romans 3:29-30].

"Therefore concerning the eating of things offered to idols, we know that an idol is nothing in the world, and that there is no other God but one." (1 Corinthians 8:4).

"Now a mediator does not mediate for one only, but God is one" [Galatians 3:20].

In the book of Jude, we read:

> [24] To him who is able to keep you from stumbling and to present you before his glorious presence without fault and with great joy—[25] to the only God our Savior be glory, majesty, power and authority, through Jesus Christ our Lord, before all ages, now and forevermore! Amen [Jude 1:24].

A glance at the Scriptures reveals that: There is only One God:

- *"Yahweh, He is God; there is no other besides Him"* [Deuteronomy 4:35].
- "Yahweh, He is God in heaven above and on the earth below; there is no other" [Deuteronomy 4:39].
- "See now that I, I am He, And there is no god besides Me" [Deuteronomy 32:39]
- "Hear, O Israel! Yahweh is our God, Yahweh is one [echad]!" [Deuteronomy 6:4].
- "You are great, O Lord God; for there is none like You, and there is no God besides You" [2 Samuel 7:22].

- "For who is God, besides Yahweh? And who is a rock, besides our God?" [2 Samuel 22:32]
- "Yahweh is God; there is no one else." 1 Kings 8:60
- "O Lord, there is none like You, nor is there any God besides You" 1 Chronicles 17:20
- "You alone [bad] are Yahweh." Nehemiah 9:6
- "For who is God, but Yahweh? And who is a rock, except our God" Psalm 18:31
- "You alone [bad], Lord, are God." Isaiah 37:20
- "Before Me there was no God formed, And there will be none after Me." Isaiah 43:10
- "'I am the first and I am the last, And there is no God besides Me." Isaiah 44:6
- "Is there any God besides Me, Or is there any *other* Rock? I know of none." Isaiah 44:8
- "I am Yahweh, and there is no other; Besides Me there is no God." Isaiah 45:5
- "Surely, God is with you, and there is none else, No other God." Isaiah 45:14
- "I am Yahweh, and there is none else." Isaiah 45:18
- "Is it not I, Yahweh? And there is no other God besides Me, A righteous God and a Savior; There is none except Me." Isaiah 45:21
- "I am God, and there is no other; *I am* God, and there is no one like Me" Isaiah 46:9
- "But do not be called Rabbi; for One [hen] is your Teacher, and you are all brothers." Matthew 23:8
- "Do not be called leaders; for One [hen] is your Leader, that is, Christ." Matthew 23:10
- ""The foremost is, 'Hear, O Israel! The Lord our God is one [hen] Lord; "Mark 12:29
- "you do not seek the glory that is from the one and only [monos] God?" John 5:44
- *"I and the Father are one [hen]." John 10:30*
- *"This is eternal life, that they may know You, the only [monos] true God" John 17:3*
- *"The glory which You have given Me I have given to them, that they may be one [hen], just as We are one* [hen]*" John 17:22*
- "since indeed God is one [hen]" Romans 3:30

- "to the only [monos] wise God, Amen." Romans 16:27
- "there is no God but one [hen]" 1 Corinthians 8:4
- "yet for us there is *but* one [hen] God, the Father, from whom are all things
- and we *exist* for Him; and one [hen] Lord, Jesus Christ, by whom are all things, and we *exist* through Him." 1 Corinthians 8:6
- "Now a mediator is not for one *party only;* whereas God is *only* one [hen]." Galatians 3:20

These passages from the Scriptures and several others testify to the Oneness of God, The Triune WHO is the Father, The Son and the Holy Spirit.

It is obvious that many prophets and disciples believe that there is Only One God and their testimonies can help to strengthen our faith. The question is to determine Who that God Is. When we read passages of the Scriptures as [John 1:1-5], it becomes clear who the Creator is, and we are instructed that He was the Word in the beginning and He was with God and He was God. Obviously, this is the Lord Jesus Christ because the Lord Jesus Christ is the Word that became Flesh. Most scholars including Philip Johnson believes that the passage of John 1:1-5 clearly tells us who the Creator is.

In his discussion about defeating the theory of evolution, Phillip E. Johnson states that the passage of John 1:1-5 is the most powerful passage of the Scriptures that teaches about creation and that points us to the Creator, this passage tells us clearly who the Creator Is.

Now, we can choose to dismiss what Phillip Johnson says and seek to find what the LORD Jesus Christ Himself says about Who He Is. One can choose to ignore what others say about the Lord Jesus Christ and seek to raise challenges. But what about what the Lord Jesus Christ says about Himself?

Clearly, the Lord teaches that there is Only One God:

29 "The most important one," answered Jesus, "is this: 'Hear, O Israel: The Lord our God, the Lord is one.[c] [Mark 12:29]. The

Lord also taught that He and the father are One: [30] I and the Father are one" [John 10:30].

Now, that we know that there is Only One God, the question is to identify the Only One God. What are the names and the titles of the Only One God Scriptures teach us about?

Who Is God of the Bible and What are His Names? Only Scriptures can help us to answer these questions properly.

For examples, powerful passages in the Book of John 1:1-14 and powerful Passages in the Book of Colossians [1:15-20], teach us about the True God.

When we read the passages of the Scriptures like [John 1:1-5], it becomes clear to see who the Creator Is, as we are instructed that He was the Word in the beginning, and He was with God and He was God. Obviously this is the Lord Jesus Christ because the Lord Jesus Christ is the Word that became Flesh. Most scholars including Philip Johnson believe that the passage of John 1-1-5 clearly points to the Creator [Defeating Darwinism By Open Minds (1997).

3. The Premises of Logic.

The premises of logic illumines the mind and shades lights on such complex concepts as Trinity, God's Truth, God's Power and God's Glory. The premises of logic guide the minds to think over premises and draw logical conclusions that make sense and basically imply the truth of a statement. In this session, we will present arguments that will help us to evaluate the reliability of inferences, which are the patterns of reasoning that go from premises to conclusion in a logical argument as most thinkers would agree. Since the main models to consider in most logical arguments are deductive argument and inductive argument, the first deriving from general to particular and the later from particular to general, we will examine truth and validity from the perspectives of deductive argument instead of inductive argument. According to logic, a deductive argument is said to be valid when the inference from premises to conclusion is perfect. In other words, if the premises of a valid argument are true, then its conclusion must also be true. It is impossible for the conclusion of a valid argument to be false when the premises are true. Let us read and reason as were read premises in the following lines:

- If Scriptures teach that there is Only One God
- and God states that, He will Never share His glory with Another
- Therefore, there is Only One God

- If the Lord Jesus Christ states that He and the Father are One
- And if the Father calls Jesus Christ God,
- Therefore, Jesus Christ is The Only True God.

- If Scriptures teach that there is Only One Savior and He is God
- And Jesus Christ teaches that He is the Savior of the World
- Therefore, God is Jesus Christ, the Savior of the world.

The Premises of logic about Christ's Deity can be supported more by the following verses:

- Revelation 1:7-8 Jesus was the Almighty.
- Genesis 17:1 And the Almighty was God.

    Therefore, Jesus Christ is the Almighty God

- John 8:58 Jesus was the "I Am"
- Exodus 3:14 and the "I Am" was God

    Therefore, Jesus is God the I Am"

- Acts 3:14 Jesus was the "HOLY ONE"
- Isaiah 43:15 and the "HOLY ONE" was God

    Therefore, Jesus is the HOLY ONE

- John 8:24 Jesus is the "I Am He"
- Isaiah 43:10 and the "I Am He" was God

Therefore, Jesus is the I Am He, and the I Am He IS God.

- Revelation 22:13 Jesus is the "First and the Last"
- Isaiah 44:6 and the "First and the Last" was God

Therefore, Jesus is God

- I Corinthians 10:4 Jesus was "The Rock"
- Psalm 18:31 and "The Rock" was God

Therefore, Jesus is God

Other Scriptures to consider for critical thinking include the following:

- Hosea 13:4 I am Jehovah your God, there was no God except me, and there was no savior but I.
- Joel 2:27 I am your God, and None Else
- Zechariah 14:9 In that day shall there be ONE LORD AND HIS NAME ONE
- Philippians 2:11 that Jesus Christ is Lord, to the Glory of God the Father
- Matthew 23:9 For one is your Father, the heavenly one
- Mark 12:29 Jehovah our God is one Jehovah.

Also, Paul in the Book of Corinthians, refers to The Only One God.

> "Therefore concerning the eating of things offered to idols, we know that an idol is nothing in the world, and that there is no other God but one" [1 Corinthians 8:4].

"Now a mediator does not mediate for one only, but God is one" [Galatians 3:20].

In the Book of Jude, we read about the Only One God.

> Scriptures refers to the Lord Jesus Christ as the Creator of the universe:

The Word Became Flesh:

[1] In the beginning was the Word, and the Word was with God, and the Word was God. [2] He was with God in the beginning. [3] Through him all things were made; without him nothing was made that has been made. [4] In him was life, and that life was the light of all mankind. [5] The light shines in the darkness, and the darkness has not overcome[a] it [John 1:1-5].

- God Who created the universe [Colossians 1:1-15].
- God our Creator, God Who created all [John1:1-14].

[1] In the beginning . . . . full of grace and truth [John 1:1-14].

[Hebrews 1:1-6] And again, oil of joy

Colossians 1:1-15 The Supremacy of the Son of God

[15] The Son is the image of the invisible God, the firstborn over all creation. [16] For in him all things were created: things in heaven and on earth,

Does everyone believe that?

We need to pray to God and ask Him to teach us about Himself, to help us believe in Him, and to seek to understand His nature and His will and we need to believe in the Scriptures because Scriptures are the breathed Word of God [2 Timothy 3: 16]. Scriptures teach that God created the the world and that without faith, it is impossible to please God [Hebrews 11:6]. Furthermore, the Lord instructs us that: Heavens and Earth will pass away, but not His word. [Matthew 25:35].

Jesus is God—Prophecies

- *The Divine Messiah was Predicted in the Old Testament.*
  Isaiah 7:14: *"Therefore the Lord himself will give you a sign: The virgin will be with child and will give birth to a son, and will call him Immanuel."[1]* "Immanuel" exactly means: "God with us." As we also read in the Book of Matthew 1:23; Jesus was "God with us."

- *This Messiah would be born a human son, but have a higher nature.* Isaiah 9:6: *"For to us a child is born, to us a son is given, and the government will be on his shoulders. And He will be called Wonderful Counselor, Mighty God, Everlasting Father, Prince of Peace."* This was a radical statement by monotheistic Jewish prophet who called a human being "Mighty God"; and God fulfilled centuries later in Christ.

- *Even before in the Book of Daniel, we read about the Divine Messiah.* Daniel 7:13-14: *"There before me was one like a son of man, coming with the clouds of heaven . . . He was given authority, glory and sovereign power; all peoples, nations and men of every language worshiped him. His dominion is an everlasting dominion that will not pass away, and his kingdom is one that will never be destroyed."*

After reading, we can reject what other say about the Only One God, and the premises of logic about Christ's Deity but what about what the Lord Jesus Christ Himself teaches?

4. The teachings of our Lord and Savior Jesus Christ and His Views on the Only One True God.

The Lord taught that there is Only One God: [29]

"The most important one," answered Jesus, "is this: 'Hear, O Israel: The Lord our God, the Lord is one [Mark 12:29].

The Lord Jesus Christ claimed to be the ONLY way to God:

> John 14:6 "I am the way, the truth, and the life. No one comes to the Father but by me."
> Matthew 11:27 "All things have been . . . reveal him."

The Lord Jesus Christ claimed to have shared the glory of God in Heaven. He existed with the Father in Eternity past:

> John 17:5 "And now, Father, glorify me in your presence with the glory I had with you before the world began."

In [John 1:1-5]

The Lord Jesus Christ claimed to have the power and the ability to forgive sins:

> Luke 5:20-21 "When Jesus saw their faith, he said, 'Friend, your
> sins are forgiven
> *Luke 7:48-49 "Then Jesus said to her, 'Your sins are forgiven.'... sins?'"*

The Lord Jesus Christ claimed that He is The Unique Heavenly King:

> Luke 22:69 "But from now on, the Son of Man will be seated at
> the right hand of the mighty God."
> Luke 23:1-3 "Then . . . 'Yes, it is as you say,' Jesus replied."
> John 18:36-37 "Jesus said, 'My kingdom . . . . Everyone on the
> side of truth listens to me.'"

The Lord Jesus Christ claimed to be able to give everlasting life:

> John 6:40 "For my . . . at the last day."
> John 6:47 "I tell you the truth, he who believes has everlasting life."
> John 10:28-30 "I give . . . . I and the Father are one."
> John 11:25 "Jesus said to her, 'I am the resurrection and the life.
> will never die . . . '"

The Lord Jesus claimed that He would die and come back to life:

> John 10:17 . . . but I lay it down of my own accord.
> John 12:32-33 "'But I, . . . to die."
> John 16:16 "In a little while you will see me no more, and then
> after a little while you will see me."
> Luke 18:31-33 "Jesus took the Twelve aside and told them, . . . he
> will rise again.'"

The Lord Jesus Christ claimed that He would return again to judge the world:

> Matthew 24:27-30 "So as the lightening . . . great glory."
> Matthew 25:31-32 "When the Son of Man . . . the goats."

> Mark 14:61-62 "Again the high priest asked him, . . . of heaven.'"

Once, the Lord said that before Moses was, He was [John 5:58]:

Elsewhere the Lord Jesus Christ said that there is Only One God [Mark 12:29], just as we read in other passages of the Scriptures including [Deuteronomy 6:4], [Isaiah 45:22], [Isaiah 44:6], [Isaiah 45:18], [Isaiah 45:6], [Isaiah 48:11] and [Isaiah 43:10-11] to mention these.

The Lord also says that He is the way the Truth and Life [John 14:6]

Later, the Lord admonished His audience that if they did not believe that He Was Who He said that He was, They would perish in their sins. This warning by the LORD, also applies to us.

What can we do? Shall we choose to believe in the LORD's own words and accept Him as our personal savior or shall we reject the LORD Jesus Christ and perish in our sins?

Jesus Christ said that He is Eternal Life and that He gives eternal life. He also teaches that there is hell and heavens and that those who accept him will spend eternity with him in heaven:

> And if I go and prepare a place for you, I will come back and take you to be with me that you also may be where I am [John 14:3].

Where will you spend eternity?

The LORD says:

The Deity of Jesus Christ has been an issue of controversies, disputes and challenges. Perhaps there is no other issue that causes people to raise eye-brows and make them uncomfortable, upset and even make them angry to hear than the issue about the Deity and Sovereignty of the Lord Jesus Christ. Many people believe in God's existence and they accept that there is only one God and that God can take all forms even becoming a man and be called Jesus Christ. However, others believe in God's existence and worship God as the Creator, the Maker of the universe, but the only problem they have is that, God the Creator, the Maker of the heavens and the earth, Master of the universe could not take a human form and became a Human being to live on earth and be called Lord Jesus Christ; even though Scriptures said that the Baby Jesus was called Immanuel which means God with us. That's impossible, one would say, even though Scripture teach that nothing is impossible with God. Let us pause and think for a while, if everything is possible with God, and if God is God of impossibility, why wouldn't it be possible for God to form a human body and become Man? The challenge many face is not to believe in the impossibility of God, but to believe in Jesus Christ and to surrender to His authority. The Lord says that He has all Authority, ". . . *All authority in heaven and on earth has been given to me.* [19]Therefore go and make disciples of all nations, baptizing them in[a] the name of the Father and of the Son and of the Holy Spirit, [20]and teaching them to obey everything I have commanded you. And surely I am with you always, to the very end of the age" [Matthew 28:16-20].

Believing in God's existence is not an issue per se, this is not an issue at the stake because many peoples believe in God's existence, and many worship God, the issue is to believe in the humility of God as God decided to take on flesh to become Human. On Humility of Christ the apostle Paul writes:

> [5]Your attitude should be the same as that of Christ Jesus:
> [6]Who, being in very nature[a] God, did not consider equality with God something to be grasped,
> [7]but made himself nothing, taking the very nature[b] of a servant, being made in human likeness.
> [8]And being found in appearance as a man, he humbled himself and became obedient to death—even death on a cross!
> [9]Therefore God exalted him to the highest place and gave him the name that is above every name,
> [10]that at the name of Jesus every knee should bow, in heaven and on earth and under the earth,
> [11]and every tongue confess that Jesus Christ is Lord, to the glory of God the Father [Philippians 2:5—11].

Annie Ngana-Mundeke (Ph.D).

On believing in God, James writes that all knee shall bow and everything confess that Jesus Christ is LORD to the glory of God the Father. It seems that the issue is not to believe in God, but to surrender to Christ's authority as Paul teaches:

> [19]You believe that there is one God. Good! Even the demons believe that—and shudder [James 1: 17].

The teachings of our Lord and Savior Jesus Christ and His views on the Only One True God. Clearly, reveals the Lord Jesus Christ's claim of His Deity, [Mark 12:29] and [John 10:30].

Despite the witnesses from so many, some still reject the fact that there is Only One God. However, others simply dismiss the fact that God exists and dismiss the the issue of creation, the Fall of man, sins and salvation and choose to live with consequences:

> [16] For God so loved the world that he gave his one and only Son, that whoever believes in him shall not perish but have eternal life. [17] For God did not send his Son into the world to condemn the world, but to save the world through him. [18] Whoever believes in him is not condemned, but whoever does not believe stands condemned already because they have not believed in the name of God's one and only Son [John 3:16-17].

Discussing God's existence and stating that God created the world makes some people angry, but stating that God and Jesus Christ are one and that Jesus Christ is God the Creator, makes people even more angry

With this in mind, we can see the difficulties many may face.

The Lord Jesus Christ also stated that He has all authority, and He is The Alpha and the Omega

The LORD even admonishes us that if we do not believe that he is who he says he is, we will perish:

I told you that you would die in your sins; if you do not believe that I am he, you will indeed die in your sins" [John 8:24].

For his part the apostle Paul provides us with powerful passages regarding the Supremacy of Christ when he writes:

> [15] He is the image of the invisible God, the firstborn over all creation. [16]For by him all things were created: things in heaven and on earth, visible and invisible, whether thrones or powers or rulers or authorities; all things were created by him and for him.

> [17] He is before all things, and in him all things hold together. [18]And he is the head of the body, the church; he is the beginning and the firstborn from among the dead, so that in everything he might have the supremacy. [19]For God was pleased to have all his fullness dwell in him, [20]and through him to reconcile to himself all things, whether things on earth or things in heaven, by making peace through his blood, shed on the cross [Colossians 1:15-20].

Only God, our Creator could have mercy to come to earth to save us, His Peoples; No one else can love us more than God does. God created us in His image. God has mercy for us and He came to save us after the Fall [Genesis 3]. What do you think of the following passages from the Scriptures, the word of God [Genesis 3: 19—24 and [John 1:29]?

> [19] By the sweat of your brow you will eat your food until you return to the ground, since from it you were taken; for dust you are and to dust you will return."

> [20] Adam [c] named his wife Eve, [d] because she would become the mother of all the living.

> [21] The LORD God made garments of skin for Adam and his wife and clothed them. [22] And the LORD God said, "The man has now become like one of us, knowing good and evil. He must not be allowed to reach out his hand and take also from the tree of life and

eat, and live forever." [23] So the LORD God banished him from the Garden of Eden to work the ground from which he had been taken. [24] After he drove the man out, he placed on the east side [c] of the Garden of Eden cherubim and a flaming sword flashing back and forth to guard the way to the tree of life [Genesis 3: 19—24]?

Jesus the Lamb of God

[29]The next day John saw Jesus coming toward him and said, "Look, the Lamb of God, who takes away the sin of the world! [30]This is the one I meant when I said, 'A man who comes after me has surpassed me because he was before me.' [31]I myself did not know him, but the reason I came baptizing with water was that he might be revealed to Israel." [John 1:29]?

Conclusion

There is only One God, and as Scriptures teach us and confirm that the Lord Jesus Christ is God our Creator. The Lord Jesus Christ teaches that there is Only One God and that He and the Father are One: "I and the Father are one" [John 10:30].

Activities for this chapter.

1. Write down the passages that teach that there is only One God.

_____

_____

_____

_____

2. Which of the passages you have cited deal with the Deity of the LORD Jesus Christ?

_____

_____

_____

_____

3. Which of the passage (s) you have cited seems or seem to sound more convincing or seem to minister to you the most?

_____

_____

_____

_____

Some people believe that during His Earthly ministry, the Lord Jesus Christ revealed Himself powerfully and that in instance such as when He said: "The Father and I are One," "I am" and even when He accepted to be worshiped, and He spoke to the winds and Nature obeyed Him; these instances and many others powerfully demonstrate the Deity of the LORD Jesus as God the Creator. Write down the passages that relate such critical instances and write down in a sentence or two sentences what you think of these instances.

_____

_____

_____

_____

If these instances convince you of the Deity of the LORD Jesus Christ that The LORD Jesus is indeed God, Our Creator or if you were already sure that the LORD Jesus Christ is God our Creator and that He created the heavens and the earth smile, rejoice, praise the LORD and make a list of friends and relatives you would like to share this awesome truth with.

Write down their names and make it your mission to share with them and pray that the LORD opens their minds to know who He is and to accept Him as their Creator and their savior.

_____

_____

_____

_____

CHAPTER 4

Lord Jesus Christ, God Almighty

"I am the Alpha and the Omega," says the Lord God, "who is, and who was, and who is to come, the Almighty"[Revelation 1:8].

Can one be Almighty and not be God the Creator? There is Only One God as Scriptures teach us"[Revelation 1:8].

Having recognized that there is Only One God, we need also to read about what God says about sharing His glory. Throughout the Scriptures, the Word of God teaches that God will never share His glory with anyone as we can read in the following passages:

> "I am the LORD; that is my name!
> I will not yield my glory to another
> or my praise to idols [Isaiah 42:8].

Moreover, other passages such as the passage of Deuteronomy, the LORD teaches that there is Only One God: Hear, O Israel: The LORD our God, the LORD is one. [Deuteronomy 6: 4].

As we can observe Scriptures are clear on the fact that there is Only One God, there is no way to deny this truth.

Christ's Deity is an issue of heated debates, but Scriptures, the inspired word of God instruct us repeatedly that there is Only One God and He is the Almighty as we read in the Book of [Revelation 1:8] and in several other passages.

Many passages in Scriptures in the Holy Bible teach us about the Deity of the Lord Jesus Christ and confirm that the Lord Jesus Christ is God, Our

Creator because the Lord created everything, and He is the Almighty God and angels worship Him. Consider for examples the following passages from the Scriptures:

- In the beginning was the word, and the Word was with God, and the Word was God.
- Wonderful Counselor, [b] Mighty God, Everlasting Father, Prince of Peace.

As we can notice in the above passage, the Lord Jesus Christ is called God Almighty. The Lord Jesus Christ is called mighty God. Several Scriptures teach that the LORD Jesus God is God Almighty:

- Isaiah 9:6 as we just read:

  ^{6} For to us a child is born,
  to us a son is given,
  and the government will be on his shoulders.
  And he will be called
  Wonderful Counselor, Mighty God,
  Everlasting Father, Prince of Peace.

This passage which was a prophecy about the coming of the Lord to earth had challenged many minds as they could not accept that the Lord is God.

The Lord told his disciples that He and the Father are One and that He who saw Him, saw the father:

- [John 14:6-7].

- [John 10:30].

- Scriptures teach that the Lord Jesus Christ is God:

  The Word Became Flesh

  ^{1} In the beginning was the Word, and the Word was with God, and the Word was God. ^{2} He was with God in the beginning. ³ Through him all things were made; without him nothing was made that has been made. ⁴ In him was life, and that life was the light of all mankind. ⁵ The light shines in the darkness, and the darkness has not overcome[a] it.

⁶ There was a man sent from God whose name was John. ⁷ He came as a witness to testify concerning that light, so that through him all might believe. ⁸ He himself was not the light; he came only as a witness to the light.

⁹ The true light that gives light to everyone was coming into the world. ¹⁰ He was in the world, and though the world was made through him, the world did not recognize him. ¹¹ He came to that which was his own, but his own did not receive him. ¹² Yet to all who did receive him, to those who believed in his name, he gave the right to become children of God—¹³ children born not of natural descent, nor of human decision or a husband's will, but born of God.

¹⁴ The Word became flesh and made his dwelling among us. We have seen his glory, the glory of the one and only Son, who came from the Father, full of grace and truth [John 1:1-14].

¹ In the beginning was the Word, and the Word was with God, and the Word was God. ² [John 1:1].

- Also, John's first epistle refers to Jesus Christ in the same way,

"That which was from the beginning, which we have heard, which we have seen with our eyes, which we have looked upon, and our hands have handled, of the Word of life . . ." [1 John 1:1].

- Later, in this same epistle, we read that 1 John 5:20, "And we know that the Son of God is come, and hath given us an understanding, that we may know him that is true, and we are in him that is true, even in his Son Jesus Christ. This is the true God, and eternal life."

- For His part, Thomas called the Lord My God: [John 14:]

- Colossians 2:9 reads: "For in him (Christ) dwelleth all the fullness of the Godhead bodily."

- Titus 2:13, instructs: "Looking for that blessed hope, and the glorious appearing of the great God and our Savior Jesus Christ . . . ."

- 2 Corinthians 4:4 teaches: "In whom the god of this world (Satan) hath blinded the minds of them which believe not, lest the light of the glorious gospel of Christ, who is the image of God, should shine unto them."

- 1 Timothy 3:16, "And without controversy great is the mystery of godliness: God was manifest in the flesh, justified in the Spirit, seen of angels, preached unto the Gentiles, believed on in the world, received up into glory."

- 2 Corinthians 5:19, ". . . God was in Christ, reconciling the world unto himself . . . ." So Jesus Christ was God manifesting Himself in the flesh, reconciling the world to Himself.

- 1:23 says, "Behold, a virgin shall be with child, and shall bring forth a son, and they shall call his name Emmanuel, which being interpreted is, God with us."

In the beginning the Lord God said, "Let make man in our image" [Genesis 2:27]. Most scholars believe that Elohim implied plurality:

Genesis 1:1, "In the beginning God created the heaven and the earth." The word translated as "God" is "Elohim" in the original Hebrew which is a plural word. It occurs more than 2000 times in the Old Testament. Another example is Genesis 1:26 which says, "And God said, Let us make man in our image, after our likeness . . . .

Other passages that express the plurality of God include;

Genesis 11:7, ". . . let us go down, and there confound their language, that they may not understand one another's speech." and Genesis 3:22 says, "And the LORD God said, Behold, the man is become as one of us, to know good and evil . . . . name "Jesus" is the Greek form of the Hebrew word yeh-ho-shoo'-ah which means "Jehovah is salvation".

So here in Genesis 3:22, *"LORD God"* is Jehovah Elohim. As a side note, the

The LORD Jesus Christ is God, Our Creator:

Hebrews 1:1-3 reads: [1] In the past God spoke to our ancestors through the prophets at many times and in various ways, [2] but in these last days he has spoken to us by his Son, whom he appointed heir of all things, and through whom also he made the universe.

God calls the Lord Jesus Christ, "God" and acknowledges that He created the heavens and the earth.

Hebrews 1:8-10 states:

[8] But about the Son he says,

"Your throne, O God, will last for ever and ever; a scepter of justice will be the scepter of your kingdom.

[9] You have loved righteousness and hated wickedness; therefore God, your God, has set you above your companions by anointing you with the oil of joy."[c]

[10] He also says,

"In the beginning, Lord, you laid the foundations of the earth, and the heavens are the work of your hands.

[11] They will perish, but you remain; they will all wear out like a garment.

[12] You will roll them up like a robe; like a garment they will be changed.

But you remain the same, and your years will never end."[f]

"Your throne, O God, will last for ever and ever; a scepter of justice will be the scepter of your kingdom.

Here, God is calling Jesus Christ "God" and accrediting Him with the creation of heaven and earth.

John 1:3 says of "*the Word*", Jesus Christ, "*All things were made by him; and without him was not anything made that was made.*"

Ephesians 3:9

"*And to make all men see what is the fellowship of the mystery, which from the beginning of the world hath been hid in God, who created all things by Jesus Christ . . . .*"

Colossians 1:14-17:

Jesus Christ is the Almighty God, the Judge and the King as we read in the book of Revelation. The Book of Revelation reveals to us much of the Nature of our Lord and Savior Jesus Christ, God, our Creator.

The Lord Jesus Christ is the Ancient of Day as He is described,

His hairs, His eyes, His clothes, all in Him refer to the Ancient of Day.

[Revelation 1:14]:

"*His head and his hairs were white like wool, as white as snow . . .*" (This identifies Jesus Christ as "*the Ancient of days*" who has "*. . . the hair of his head like the pure wool . . .*"

1:14-15, Jesus Christ is described as, ". . . *his eyes were as a flame of fire; And his feet like unto fine brass, as if they burned in a furnace . . . .*" This sounds very much like Daniel 10:6, when Daniel had the vision of a man with ". . . *his eyes as lamps of fire, and his arms and his feet like in colour to polished brass . . . .*"

The voice of Jesus Christ is most unique as well. In Revelation 1:15 it is described this way: ". . . and his voice as the sound of many waters." Compare this to Ezekiel 43:2 which says, "And, behold, the glory of the God of Israel came from the way of the east: and his voice was like a noise of many waters: and the earth shined with his glory." Ezekiel 1:24 says, ". . . I heard the noise of their wings, like the noise of great waters, as the voice of the Almighty . . . ." So who has the voice like the sound of many waters? "The God of Israel", "the Almighty", who is Jesus Christ.

Also, in the Book of Revelation, John provides numerous titles and functions of the Lord Jesus Christ, as God Almighty, God our Creator, the First and the Last; the Beginning and the End, the Alpha and the Omega, and parallelism can be traced with passages from the Old Testament.

The first and the last: In several places in the Book of Revelation, Jesus Christ is called "*the First and the Last*", "*the Beginning and the Ending*", and the "*Alpha and Omega*". This is what Jehovah is often called in the Old Testament. In Revelation 1:17-18, Jesus Christ says to John, ". . . *Fear not; I am the first and the last: I am*

Revelation 1:7-8 says, "*Behold, he cometh with clouds; and every eye shall see him, and they also which pierced him, and all kindreds of the earth shall wail because of him. Even so, Amen. I am Alpha and Omega, the beginning and the ending, saith the Lord, which is, and which was, and which is to come, the Almighty.*" In

Revelation 2:8 reads: "*And unto the angel of the church in Smyrna write; These things saith the first and the last, which was dead, and is alive . . . .*"

Revelation 22:13, Jesus Christ says, "*I am the Alpha and Omega, the beginning and the end, the first and the last.*" Parallelism with Isaiah 48:12, "*Hearken unto me, O Jacob and Israel, my called; I am he; I am the first, I also am the last.*" and Isaiah 44:6, "*Thus saith the LORD* (Jehovah) *the King of Israel, and his redeemer the LORD of hosts; I am the first, and I am the last; and beside me there is no God.*"

Isaiah 41:4 says, "*Who hath wrought and done it, calling the generations from the beginning? I the LORD, the first, and with the last; I am he.*" So, when Jesus Christ keeps proclaiming "*I am the first and the last*", He wants that all of us to know that He is the Lord God of the Old Testament, the Alpha and Omega, the one who spoke the heaven and earth into being, the one who searches hearts and minds.

The LORD Jesus Christ is Spirit and He lives in the heart and He reins in the heart:

Revelation 2:23 says, ". . . I am he which searcheth the reins (minds) and hearts: and I will give unto every one of you according to your works." Parallelism with Jeremiah 17:10 which says:

"I the LORD (Jehovah) search the heart, I try the reins, even to give every man according to his ways, and according to the fruit of his doings." Who does this? "The LORD". So we see then that Jesus Christ is Jehovah, the Almighty God, the one speaking in the Old Testament. Also, Psalms 44:21 reads: "Shall not God search this out? for he knoweth the secrets of the heart."

His return will be majestic; His return is the return of God because Scriptures describe the LORD as the King and the Judge WHO will return to judge His peoples, the living and the dead. Fort example, the Book of Acts 1:9-12 teaches us that, ". . . while they beheld, he was taken up; and a cloud received him out of their sight. And while they looked stedfastly toward heaven as he went up, behold, two men stood by them in white apparel; Which also said, Ye men of Galilee, why stand ye gazing up into heaven? this same Jesus, which is taken up from you into heaven, shall so come in like manner as ye have seen him go into heaven. Then returned they unto Jerusalem from the mount called Olivet . . . ." So we know that when Jesus Christ returns to earth, He will descend from the sky to the Mount of Olives.

- Zechariah 14:3-4
- Isaiah 45:22-23 says:
- Philippians 2:10-11

As we can notice, the LORD Jesus Christ is God Almighty, God our Creator.

Jesus Christ is the Creator of heaven and earth, the First and the Last, the Alpha and the Omega, the Beginning and the End, the Ancient of Days, God of Israel, Jehovah, the Savior, the Everlasting Father, the Almighty God.

If anyone has doubt, he or she can ask the LORD to reveal Himself to her or to him. The Lord Jesus Christ reveals Himself to peoples. The LORD says that apart from Him, we cannot do anything. The Lord also says that the Holy Spirit teaches about Him:

> "All this I have spoken while still with you. ²⁶ But the Advocate, the Holy Spirit, whom the Father will send in my name, will teach you all things and will remind you of everything I have said to you [[John 14:25-26]

John the Baptist denies being the Christ because He was not Christ. Christ is God our Creator. Even Satan recognizes Christ's Deity as we read in the Book of John during the temptation.

John came to earth to prepare the way for God to come to earth[John 1: 29]. Similarly, in the Book of Isaiah, we read that the way was being prepared for the Messiah:

> ³ The voice of one crying in the wilderness:
> "Prepare the way of the LORD;
> Make straight in the desert[a]
> A highway for our God [Isaiah 40:3].

In the Book of Isaiah, we read that the Lord Jesus Christ is God Almighty, Mighty God.

> For unto us a Child is born, unto us a Son is given; and the government shall be upon His shoulder. And His name shall be called Wonderful, Counselor, The Mighty God, The Everlasting Father, The Prince of Peace [Isaiah 9:6].

> Thomas said to him, "My Lord and my God!" [John 20:28].

[16]And without controversy great is the mystery of godliness: God was manifest in the flesh, justified in the Spirit, seen of angels, preached unto the Gentiles, believed on in the world, received up into glory [1 Timothy 3:16] KJM version

I and the Father are one [John 10:30].

Also, Hebrews [1:8—10] instructs us about Christ's Deity:

- [Philippians 2:5-11].

- And we know that the Son of God has come and has given us an understanding, that we may know Him who is true; and we are in Him who is true, in His Son Jesus Christ. This is the true God and eternal life [1 John 5:20].KJ

- [7]For there are three that bear witness in heaven: the Father, the Word, and the Holy Spirit; and these three are one [1 John 5:7]. KJ

- [28]*Keep watch over yourselves and all the flock of which the Holy Spirit has made you overseers.[a] Be shepherds of the church of God,[b] which he bought with his own blood* [Acts 20:28].

- [16]This is how we know what love is: Jesus Christ laid down his life for us. And we ought to lay down our lives for our brothers [1John 3:16].

- [59] And they stoned Stephen as he was calling on *God* and saying, "Lord Jesus, receive my spirit [Acts 7:59]

Jesus is the Way to the Father:

[John 14-5-9].

Before He ascended to heaven, the LORD says:

"All authority in heaven and on earth has . . . to the very end of the age" [Matthew 28:18-19].

Conclusion

The Lord Jesus Christ is God Almighty as He says, the Lord Jesus Christ is, *El Shaddai*: The Lord God Almighty as He says "I am Almighty God; walk before Me and be blameless." Genesis 17:1. Scriptures teach that "He who dwells in the secret place of the Most High shall abide under the shadow of the Almighty" [Psalm 91:1].

Activities for this Chapter:

1. Who is the Almighty God?

_____

_____

_____

_____

2. Cite Scriptures that teach that the Lord Jesus Christ is God Almighty

_____

_____

_____

_____

CHAPTER 5

The LORD Jesus Christ, Creator of heavens and earth.

He is the image of the invisible God, the firstborn over all creation. [16]For by him all things were created: things in heaven and on earth, visible and invisible, whether thrones or powers or rulers or authorities; all things were created by him and for him. [17]He is before all things, and in him all things hold together [Colossians 1:15].

Who Is the Creator? What do Scriptures teach about Him?

A glance at the Scriptures in the Holy Bible reveals that there is Only One God who has specific attributes that are assigned Only to Him, God Jehovah, the Great I am. These attributes include omniscience, omnipotence, omnipresence [Psalms 139]. God is Omniscient, He knows everything including the thoughts in man's heart [Matthew 9:4]. God is omnipotent, He is Almighty [Revelation 1:8]. God is Omnipresence, He is everywhere [Psalms 139]. These attributes refer to the Lord Jesus Christ and teach as that there is Only One God

"You are my witnesses," declares the LORD, "and my servant whom I have chosen, so that you may know and believe me and understand that I am he. Before me no god was formed, nor will there be one after me," (Isaiah 43:10).

Jesus		God
John 1:3, "Through him all things were made; without him nothing was made that has been made."		Job 33:4, "The Spirit of God has made me; the breath of the Almighty gives me life."
Col. 1:16-17, "For by him all things were created: things in heaven and on earth, visible and invisible, whether thrones or powers or rulers or authorities; all things were created by him and for him. He is before all things, and in him all things hold together."	Creator	Isaiah 40:28, "Do you not know? Have you not heard? The LORD is the everlasting God, the Creator of the ends of the earth. He will not grow tired or weary, and his understanding no one can fathom."

A glance at this table reveals that there is only On God, Just as the Lord Jesus Christ Jesus stated in His preaching:[29] "The most important one," answered Jesus, "is this: 'Hear, O Israel: The Lord our God, the Lord is one.[e] [Mark 1:29]

In addition, God has never sinned, and the Lord Jesus Christ has never sinned, Therefore, the Lord Jesus Christ, is God Our Creator for there is Only One God.

- Moreover, Scriptures describe theLord Jesus Christ as the Eternal God and Creator. For examples in the following passages:

Psalms 102:24-27: I said, O my God, take me not away in the midst of my days: thy years are throughout all generations. Of old hast thou laid the foundation of the earth: and the heavens are the work of thy hands. They shall perish, but thou shalt endure: yea, all of them shall wax old like a garment; as a vesture shalt thou change them, and they shall be changed: But thou art the same, and thy years shall have no end.

Hebrews 1:8 But unto the Son he saith, Thy throne, O God, is for ever and ever: a sceptre of righteousness is the sceptre of thy kingdom.

Hebrews 1:10-12 And, Thou, Lord, in the beginning hast laid the foundation of the earth; and the heavens are the works of thine hands: They shall perish; but thou remainest; and they all shall wax old as doth a garment; And as a vesture shalt thou fold them up, and they shall be changed: but thou art the same, and thy years shall not fail.

These passages from the Scriptures point to the LORD Jesus Christ as Jehovah, our Creator, the Creator of the heavens and the earth, the Creator of the Universe. The Lord Jesus Christ is the Word that become Flesh.

The Word Became Flesh [John 1:1-14].

The Lord came to earth to save us. His precious Blood was the Blood of God and it was shared for the forgiveness of our sins: [Acts 20:28]; Luke 22:20; Mark 14:24].

We are to believe in this truth. The Lord Jesus Christ says that He is the truth [John 17:3].

Several other passages in Scriptures teach us the LORD Jesus Christ is God, Our Creator. For examples, the Lord Jesus is called God, Almighty: [20] Here I am! I stand at the door and knock. If anyone hears my voice and opens the door, I will come in and eat with that person, and they with me [Revelation 3:20].

Moreover, one of His Disciples called Him LORD and God: [Hebrews 1:1-6].

The Lord told Philip that He who has seen Him has seen the Father [John 14:8-9

The LORD said to His disciples that He and His Father are One
I and the Father are one" [John10:30]. Other passages that teach us about
Christ's Deity include:

". . . CHRIST, who is the IMAGE OF GOD . . ." [II Corinthians 4:4].

". . . glory of GOD in the FACE OF JESUS CHRIST." [II Corinthians 4:6].

"GOD . . . hath in these last days spoken unto us by his SON . . . who
being the brightness of his glory, and the EXPRESS IMAGE OF HIS
PERSON . . ." [Hebrews 1:1-3].

Two passages that can be cited here in regards to Christ's Deity are the
passage of John [1:1-14] and the passage of Colossians [1:15-20].

The Lord Jesus is God our Creator, He was 100% God, 100% Man, in
Him dwelled all the fullness of Deity. Also by His name Immanuel, which
means God with us, one can start to realize that the LORD Jesus Christ is
God, our Creator indeed as there is Only One God.

The Lord Jesus Christ came to earth to save us, the peoples He created [Matthew
1:2-17].

Among many other powerful passages in the Scriptures that explain that
the Lord Jesus Christ is God, our Creator are the passages of Colossians
where we read that Christ created everything and that everything exists
through Him and by Him: [Colossians 1:15].

Moreover, in the Book of Hebrews, Scriptures teach that the Lord Jesus
Christ receives all the glory and God calls Him God:

> And again, when God brings his firstborn into the world, he says,
> "Let all God's angels worship him." [Hebrews 1:6].

In His teachings, the LORD taught that He is God, our Creator [Luke
8:24]. Scriptures teach that the LORD Jesus Christ is Eternal God, our
Creator.

• As the Eternal God and Creator.

Psalms 102:24-27 I said, O my God, take me not away in the midst of my days: thy years *are* throughout all generations. Of old hast thou laid the foundation of the earth: and the heavens *are* the work of thy hands. They shall perish, but thou shalt endure: yea, all of them shall wax old like a garment; as a vesture shalt thou change them, and they shall be changed: But thou *art* the same, and thy years shall have no end.

Hebrews 1:8 But unto the Son *he saith*, Thy throne, O God, *is* for ever and ever: a sceptre of righteousness *is* the sceptre of thy kingdom.

Hebrews 1:10-12 And, Thou, Lord, in the beginning hast laid the foundation of the earth; and the heavens are the works of thine hands: They shall perish; but thou remainest; and they all shall wax old as doth a garment; And as a vesture shalt thou fold them up, and they shall be changed: but thou art the same, and thy years shall not fail.

Conclusion

The Lord Jesus Christ is God, our Creator. He has never sinned, He went to the cross to die for our sins and He rose Himself from the dead to give us life. The Lord gave His Precious Life and shed His Precious Blood, the Blood of God to save us [Acts 20:28]. The Lord shared His precious Blood for the forgiveness of our sins [Luke 22:20; Mark 14:24].

[28] Keep watch over yourselves and all the flock of which the Holy Spirit has made you overseers. Be shepherds of the church of God,[a] which he bought with his own blood. [Acts 20:28].

Activities for This Chapter

1. Do you believe God exists?

Yes

No.

2. If you believe that God exists, your answers to the first question is "yes." Now, if you have answered yes to the first question, Question, N01, please proceed to the second question, question N0.2 and provide as many names as you can that God has in Scriptures, the Holy Bible.

_____

_____

_____

_____

While you are answering, please search for such powerful titles as; The First and the Last; the Beginning and the End. The Alpha and the Omega, the Almighty. Read passages where God is called Almighty and examine how the LORD Jesus Christ is called Almighty God.

3. If you don't believe in God's existence, your answer to question No1 was "no". Now, please step out if you are indoors and examine nature, think of beautiful sky, the vegetation, the plants, the grass and the flowers around you. Then, close your eyes and ask your question how this creation came about and write your thoughts down and then read Romans 1:20].

_____

_____

_____

_____

CHAPTER 6

The Father, the Son and the Holy Spirit are ONE

For there are three that bear witness in heaven: the Father, the Word, and the Holy Spirit; and these three are one [1 John 5:7]. KJ

Scriptures are the breathed word of God and they teach us that there is Only One God. There is Only One God Who is the Father, the Son and the Holy Spirit. There is Only One God who has three functions, as the Father, as the Son and as the Holy Spirit. He is ONE.

In the discussion about Christ's Deity, it is very important to remember that there is Only ONE God and that one can attest to this fact with confidence because it is the truth from the Scriptures, the breathed word of God:

> [16] All Scripture is God-breathed and is useful for teaching, rebuking, correcting and training in righteousness [2 Timothy 3:16].

Several other passages from the Scriptures teach that there is Only One God, the Almighty God who is the Creator of the universe. Those passages include the following:

- "there is *no one like Yahweh our God*" [Exodus 8:10].

- "*Yahweh, He is God; there is no other besides Him*" [Deuteronomy 4:35].

- "*Yahweh, He is God in heaven above and on the earth below; there is no other*" [Deuteronomy 4:39].

- "See now that I, *I am He, And there is no god besides Me*" [Deuteronomy 32:39]

- *"Hear, O Israel! Yahweh is our God, Yahweh is one!"* [Deuteronomy 6:4].

- *"You are great, O Lord God; for there is none like You, and there is no God besides You"* [2 Samuel 7:22].

- *"For who is God, besides Yahweh? And who is a rock, besides our God?"* 2 [Samuel 22:32].

- "Yahweh is God; there is no one else" [1 Kings 8:60].

- "You are the God, You alone [bad], of all the kingdoms of the earth" [2 Kings 19:15].

- "O Lord, there is none like You, nor is there any God besides You" 1 [Chronicles 17:20].

- "You alone [bad] are Yahweh" [Nehemiah 9:6]

- "For who is God, but Yahweh? And who is a rock, except our God" Psalm 18:31

- "You alone [bad], Lord, are God." Isaiah 37:20

- "Before Me there was no God formed, And there will be none after Me." Isaiah 43:10

- "'I am the first and I am the last, And there is no God besides Me." Isaiah 44:6

- "Is there any God besides Me, Or is there any *other* Rock? I know of none." Isaiah 44:8

- "I am Yahweh, and there is no other; Besides Me there is no God." Isaiah 45:5

- "Surely, God is with you, and there is none else, No other God." Isaiah 45:14

- "I am Yahweh, and there is none else." Isaiah 45:18

- "Is it not I, Yahweh? And there is no other God besides Me, A righteous God and a Savior; There is none except Me." Isaiah 45:21

- "I am God, and there is no other; *I am* God, and there is no one like Me" Isaiah 46:9

- "And Yahweh will be king over all the earth; in that day Yahweh will be *the only* one [echad], and His name *the only* one[echad]." Zechariah 14:9

- "No one can serve two masters; for either he will hate the one [hen] and love the other, or he will be devoted to one [hen] and despise the other. You cannot serve God and wealth." Matthew 6:24

- "For this reason a man shall leave his father and mother and be joined to his wife, and the two shall become one [hen] flesh"? Matthew 19:5

- "But do not be called Rabbi; for One [hen] is your Teacher, and you are all brothers." Matthew 23:8

- "Do not be called leaders; for One [hen] is your Leader, that is, Christ." Matthew 23:10

- ""The foremost is, 'Hear, O Israel! The Lord our God is one [hen] Lord;" Mark 12:29

- "you do not seek the glory that is from the one and only [monos] God?" John 5:44

- "I and the Father are one [hen]." John 10:30

- "This is eternal life, that they may know You, the only [monos] true God" John 17:3

- "The glory which You have given Me I have given to them, that they may be one [hen], just as We are one [hen]" John 17:22

- "since indeed God is one [hen]" Romans 3:30

- "to the only [monos] wise God, Amen." Romans 16:27

- "there is no God but one [hen]" 1 Corinthians 8:4

- "yet for us there is *but* one [hen] God, the Father, from whom are all things and we *exist* for Him; and one [hen] Lord, Jesus Christ, by whom are all things, and we *exist* through Him." 1 Corinthians 8:6

- "Now a mediator is not for one *party only;* whereas God is *only* one [hen]." Galatians 3:20

- "There is one [hen] body and one [hen] Spirit, one [hen] hope, one [hen] Lord, one [hen] faith, one [hen] baptism, one [hen] God and Father of all who is over all and through all and in all." Ephesians 4:4-6

- "Now to the King eternal, immortal, invisible, the only [monos] God" 1 Timothy 1:17

- "which He will bring about at the proper time—He who is the blessed and only [monos] Sovereign, the King of kings and Lord of lords, who alone [monos] possesses immortality and dwells in unapproachable light, whom no man has seen or can see. To Him *be* honor and eternal dominion! Amen." 1 Timothy 6:16

- "For there is one [hen] God, *and* one mediator also between God and men, *the* man Christ Jesus," 1 Timothy 2:5

- "You believe that God is one [hen]. You do well; the demons also believe, and shudder." James 2:19

- "For certain persons deny our only [monos] Master and Lord, Jesus Christ." Jude 4

- "the only [monos] God our Savior, through Jesus Christ our Lord. Amen." Jude 25

The above passages come from the Holy Bible, the word of God and they were compiled and examined by various scholars who have studied and have discussed them.

Since there is Only ONE God as Scriptures teach us, it is very important to take a glance at the Scriptures to examine the Deity of the LORD Jesus Christ and His Position in Scriptures.

The examination of the word of God reveals that the Lord Jesus Christ has many names and titles that Only God can Have. For example the name Jehovah, God Almighty, the title Sovereign God.

The Lord Jesus is God and He is described by following names and titles:

- As Jehovah.

  Isaiah 40:3 The voice of him that crieth in the wilderness, Prepare ye the way of the LORD, make straight in the desert a highway for our God.

  Matthew 3:3 For this is he that was spoken of by the prophet Esaias, saying, The voice of one crying in the wilderness, Prepare ye the way of the Lord, make his paths straight.

- As Jehovah of glory.

  Psalms 24:7 Lift up your heads, O ye gates; and be ye lift up, ye everlasting doors; and the King of glory shall come in.

  Psalms 24:10 Who is this King of glory? The LORD of hosts, he *is* the King of glory. Selah.

  1 Corinthians 2:8 Which none of the princes of this world knew: for had they known *it*, they would not have crucified the Lord of glory.

James 2:1 My brethren, have not the faith of our Lord Jesus Christ, *the Lord* of glory, with respect of persons.

- As Jehovah, our RIGHTEOUSNESS.

Jeremiah 23:5-6 Behold, the days come, saith the LORD, that I will raise unto David a righteous Branch, and a King shall reign and prosper, and shall execute judgment and justice in the earth. In his days Judah shall be saved, and Israel shall dwell safely: and this *is* his name whereby he shall be called, THE LORD OUR RIGHTEOUSNESS.

1 Corinthians 1:30 But of him are ye in Christ Jesus, who of God is made unto us wisdom, and righteousness, and sanctification, and redemption:

- As Jehovah, above all.

Psalms 97:9 For thou, LORD, *art* high above all the earth: thou art exalted far above all gods.

John 3:31 He that cometh from above is above all: he that is of the earth is earthly, and speaketh of the earth: he that cometh from heaven is above all.

- As Jehovah, the First and the Last.

Isaiah 44:6 Thus saith the LORD the King of Israel, and his redeemer the LORD of hosts; I *am* the first, and I *am* the last; and beside me *there is* no God.

Revelation 1:17 And when I saw him, I fell at his feet as dead. And he laid his right hand upon me, saying unto me, Fear not; I am the first and the last:

Isaiah 48:12-16 Hearken unto me, O Jacob and Israel, my called; I *am* he; I *am* the first, I also *am* the last. Mine hand also hath laid the foundation of the earth, and my right hand hath spanned the

heavens: *when* I call unto them, they stand up together. All ye, assemble yourselves, and hear; which among them hath declared these *things*? The LORD hath loved him: he will do his pleasure on Babylon, and his arm *shall be on* the Chaldeans. I, *even* I, have spoken; yea, I have called him: I have brought him, and he shall make his way prosperous. Come ye near unto me, hear ye this; I have not spoken in secret from the beginning; from the time that it was, there *am* I: and now the Lord GOD, and his Spirit, hath sent me . . . .

Revelation 22:13 I am Alpha and Omega, the beginning and the end, the first and the last.

- As Jehovah's Fellow and Equal.

Zechariah 13:7 Awake, O sword, against my shepherd, and against the man *that is* my fellow, saith the LORD of hosts: smite the shepherd, and the sheep shall be scattered: and I will turn mine hand upon the little ones.

Philippians 2:6 Who, being in the form of God, thought it not robbery to be equal with God:

- As Jehovah of Hosts.

Isaiah 6:1-3 In the year that king Uzziah died I saw also the Lord sitting upon a throne, high and lifted up, and his train filled the temple. Above it stood the seraphims: each one had six wings; with twain he covered his face, and with twain he covered his feet, and with twain he did fly. And one cried unto another, and said, Holy, holy, holy, *is* the LORD of hosts: the whole earth *is* full of his glory.

John 12:41 These things said Esaias, when he saw his glory, and spake of him.

Isaiah 8:13-14 Sanctify the LORD of hosts himself; and *let* him *be* your fear, and *let* him *be* your dread. And he shall be for a

sanctuary; but for a stone of stumbling and for a rock of offence to both the houses of Israel, for a gin and for a snare to the inhabitants of Jerusalem.

1 Peter 2:8 And a stone of stumbling, and a rock of offence, *even to them* which stumble at the word, being disobedient: whereunto also they were appointed.

- As Jehovah, the Shepherd.

Isaiah 40:11 He shall feed his flock like a shepherd: he shall gather the lambs with his arm, and carry *them* in his bosom, *and* shall gently lead those that are with young.

Hebrews 13:20 Now the God of peace, that brought again from the dead our Lord Jesus, that great shepherd of the sheep, through the blood of the everlasting covenant,

- As Jehovah, for whose glory all things were created.

Proverbs 16:4 The LORD hath made all *things* for himself: yea, even the wicked for the day of evil.

Colossians 1:16 For by him were all things created, that are in heaven, and that are in earth, visible and invisible, whether *they be* thrones, or dominions, or principalities, or powers: all things were created by him, and for him:

- As Jehovah, the Messenger of the covenant.

Malachi 3:1 Behold, I will send my messenger, and he shall prepare the way before me: and the Lord, whom ye seek, shall suddenly come to his temple, even the messenger of the covenant, whom ye delight in: behold, he shall come, saith the LORD of hosts.

Mark 1:2 As it is written in the prophets, Behold, I send my messenger before thy face, which shall prepare thy way before thee.

Luke 2:27 And he came by the Spirit into the temple: and when the parents brought in the child Jesus, to do for him after the custom of the law,

- Invoked as Jehovah.

Joel 2:32 And it shall come to pass, *that* whosoever shall call on the name of the LORD shall be delivered: for in mount Zion and in Jerusalem shall be deliverance, as the LORD hath said, and in the remnant whom the LORD shall call.

Acts 2:21 And it shall come to pass, *that* whosoever shall call on the name of the Lord shall be saved.

1 Corinthians 1:2 Unto the church of God which is at Corinth, to them that are sanctified in Christ Jesus, called *to be* saints, with all that in every place call upon the name of Jesus Christ our Lord, both theirs and ours:

- As the Eternal God and Creator.

Psalms 102:24-27 I said, O my God, take me not away in the midst of my days: thy years *are* throughout all generations. Of old hast thou laid the foundation of the earth: and the heavens *are* the work of thy hands. They shall perish, but thou shalt endure: yea, all of them shall wax old like a garment; as a vesture shalt thou change them, and they shall be changed: But thou *art* the same, and thy years shall have no end.

Hebrews 1:8 But unto the Son *he saith*, Thy throne, O God, *is* for ever and ever: a sceptre of righteousness *is* the sceptre of thy kingdom.

Hebrews 1:10-12 And, Thou, Lord, in the beginning hast laid the foundation of the earth; and the heavens are the works of thine hands: They shall perish; but thou remainest; and they all shall wax old as doth a garment; And as a vesture shalt thou fold them up, and they shall be changed: but thou art the same, and thy years shall not fail.

- As the mighty God.

  Isaiah 9:6 For unto us a child is born, unto us a son is given: and the government shall be upon his shoulder: and his name shall be called Wonderful, Counsellor, The mighty God, The everlasting Father, The Prince of Peace.

- As the Great God and Saviour.

  Hosea 1:7 But I will have mercy upon the house of Judah, and will save them by the LORD their God, and will not save them by bow, nor by sword, nor by battle, by horses, nor by horsemen.

  Titus 2:13 Looking for that blessed hope, and the glorious appearing of the great God and our Saviour Jesus Christ;

- As God over all.

  Psalms 45:6-7 Thy throne, O God, *is* for ever and ever: the sceptre of thy kingdom *is* a right sceptre. Thou lovest righteousness, and hatest wickedness: therefore God, thy God, hath anointed thee with the oil of gladness above thy fellows.

- As the true God.

  Jeremiah 10:10 But the LORD *is* the true God, he *is* the living God, and an everlasting king: at his wrath the earth shall tremble, and the nations shall not be able to abide his indignation.

  1 John 5:20 And we know that the Son of God is come, and hath given us an understanding, that we may know him that is true, and we are in him that is true, *even* in his Son Jesus Christ. This is the true God, and eternal life.

- As God the Word.

  John 1:1 In the beginning was the Word, and the Word was with God, and the Word was God.

- As God, the Judge.

Ecclesiastes 12:14 For God shall bring every work into judgment, with every secret thing, whether *it be* good, or whether *it be* evil.

1 Corinthians 4:5 Therefore judge nothing before the time, until the Lord come, who both will bring to light the hidden things of darkness, and will make manifest the counsels of the hearts: and then shall every man have praise of God.

2 Corinthians 5:10 For we must all appear before the judgment seat of Christ; that every one may receive the things *done* in *his* body, according to that he hath done, whether *it be* good or bad.

2 Timothy 4:1 I charge *thee* therefore before God, and the Lord Jesus Christ, who shall judge the quick and the dead at his appearing and his kingdom;

- As Emmanuel.

Isaiah 7:14 Therefore the Lord himself shall give you a sign; Behold, a virgin shall conceive, and bear a son, and shall call his name Immanuel.

Matthew 1:23 Behold, a virgin shall be with child, and shall bring forth a son, and they shall call his name Emmanuel, which being interpreted is, God with us.

- As King of kings and Lord of lords.

Daniel 10:17 For how can the servant of this my lord talk with this my lord? for as for me, straightway there remained no strength in me, neither is there breath left in me.

Revelation 1:5 And from Jesus Christ, *who is* the faithful witness, *and* the first begotten of the dead, and the prince of the kings of the earth. Unto him that loved us, and washed us from our sins in his own blood,

Revelation 17:14 These shall make war with the Lamb, and the Lamb shall overcome them: for he is Lord of lords, and King of kings: and they that are with him *are* called, and chosen, and faithful.

- As the Holy One.

1 Samuel 2:2 *There is* none holy as the LORD: for *there is* none beside thee: neither *is there* any rock like our God.

Acts 3:14 But ye denied the Holy One and the Just, and desired a murderer to be granted unto you;

- As the Lord from heaven.

1 Corinthians 15:47 The first man *is* of the earth, earthy: the second man *is* the Lord from heaven.

- As Lord of the sabbath.

Genesis 2:3 And God blessed the seventh day, and sanctified it: because that in it he had rested from all his work which God created and made.

Matthew 12:8 For the Son of man is Lord even of the sabbath day.

- As Lord of all.

Acts 10:36 The word which *God* sent unto the children of Israel, preaching peace by Jesus Christ: (he is Lord of all:)

Romans 10:11-13 For the scripture saith, Whosoever believeth on him shall not be ashamed. For there is no difference between the Jew and the Greek: for the same Lord over all is rich unto all that call upon him. For whosoever shall call upon the name of the Lord shall be saved.

- As Son of God.

  Matthew 26:63-67 But Jesus held his peace. And the high priest answered and said unto him, I adjure thee by the living God, that thou tell us whether thou be the Christ, the Son of God. Jesus saith unto him, Thou hast said: nevertheless I say unto you, Hereafter shall ye see the Son of man sitting on the right hand of power, and coming in the clouds of heaven. Then the high priest rent his clothes, saying, He hath spoken blasphemy; what further need have we of witnesses? behold, now ye have heard his blasphemy. What think ye? They answered and said, He is guilty of death. Then did they spit in his face, and buffeted him; and others smote *him* with the palms of their hands, . . .

- As the Only-begotten Son of the Father.

  John 1:14 And the Word was made flesh, and dwelt among us, (and we beheld his glory, the glory as of the only begotten of the Father,) full of grace and truth.

  John 3:16 For God so loved the world, that he gave his only begotten Son, that whosoever believeth in him should not perish, but have everlasting life.

  John 3:18 He that believeth on him is not condemned: but he that believeth not is condemned already, because he hath not believed in the name of the only begotten Son of God.

  1 John 4:9 In this was manifested the love of God toward us, because that God sent his only begotten Son into the world, that we might live through him.

- His blood is called the blood of God.

  Acts 20:28 Take heed therefore unto yourselves, and to all the flock, over the which the Holy Ghost hath made you overseers, to feed the church of God, which he hath purchased with his own blood.

- As one with the Father.

  John 10:30 I and *my* Father are one.

  John 12:45 And he that seeth me seeth him that sent me.

  John 14:7-10 If ye had known me, ye should have known my Father also: and from henceforth ye know him, and have seen him. Philip saith unto him, Lord, shew us the Father, and it sufficeth us. Jesus saith unto him, Have I been so long time with you, and yet hast thou not known me, Philip? he that hath seen me hath seen the Father; and how sayest thou *then*, Shew us the Father? Believest thou not that I am in the Father, and the Father in me? the words that I speak unto you I speak not of myself: but the Father that dwelleth in me, he doeth the works.

  John 17:10 And all mine are thine, and thine are mine; and I am glorified in them.

- As sending the Spirit, equally with the Father.

  John 14:16 And I will pray the Father, and he shall give you another Comforter, that he may abide with you for ever;

  John 15:26 But when the Comforter is come, whom I will send unto you from the Father, *even* the Spirit of truth, which proceedeth from the Father, he shall testify of me:

- As entitled to equal honor with the Father.

  John 5:23 That all *men* should honour the Son, even as they honour the Father. He that honoureth not the Son honoureth not the Father which hath sent him.

- As Owner of all things, equally with the Father.

  John 16:15 All things that the Father hath are mine: therefore said I, that he shall take of mine, and shall shew *it* unto you.

- As unrestricted by the law of the sabbath, equally with the Father.

  John 5:17 But Jesus answered them, My Father worketh hitherto, and I work.

- As the Source of grace, equally with the Father.

  1 Thessalonians 3:11 Now God himself and our Father, and our Lord Jesus Christ, direct our way unto you.

  2 Thessalonians 2:16-17 Now our Lord Jesus Christ himself, and God, even our Father, which hath loved us, and hath given *us* everlasting consolation and good hope through grace, Comfort your hearts, and stablish you in every good word and work.

- As unsearchable, equally with the Father.

  Proverbs 30:4 Who hath ascended up into heaven, or descended? who hath gathered the wind in his fists? who hath bound the waters in a garment? who hath established all the ends of the earth? what *is* his name, and what *is* his son's name, if thou canst tell?

  Matthew 11:27 All things are delivered unto me of my Father: and no man knoweth the Son, but the Father; neither knoweth any man the Father, save the Son, and *he* to whomsoever the Son will reveal *him*.

- As Creator of all things.

  Isaiah 40:28 Hast thou not known? hast thou not heard, *that* the everlasting God, the LORD, the Creator of the ends of the earth, fainteth not, neither is weary? *there is* no searching of his understanding.

  John 1:3 All things were made by him; and without him was not anything made that was made.

Colossians 1:16 For by him were all things created, that are in heaven, and that are in earth, visible and invisible, whether *they be* thrones, or dominions, or principalities, or powers: all things were created by him, and for him:

Hebrews 1:2 Hath in these last days spoken unto us by *his* Son, whom he hath appointed heir of all things, by whom also he made the worlds;

- As Supporter and Preserver of all things.

Nehemiah 9:6 Thou, *even* thou, *art* LORD alone; thou hast made heaven, the heaven of heavens, with all their host, the earth, and all *things* that *are* therein, the seas, and all that *is* therein, and thou preservest them all; and the host of heaven worshippeth thee.

Colossians 1:17 And he is before all things, and by him all things consist.

Hebrews 1:3 Who being the brightness of *his* glory, and the express image of his person, and upholding all things by the word of his power, when he had by himself purged our sins, sat down on the right hand of the Majesty on high;

- As possessed of the fulness of the God head.

Colossians 2:9 For in him dwelleth all the fulness of the Godhead bodily.

Hebrews 1:3 Who being the brightness of *his* glory, and the express image of his person, and upholding all things by the word of his power, when he had by himself purged our sins, sat down on the right hand of the Majesty on high;

- As raising the dead.

John 5:21 For as the Father raiseth up the dead, and quickeneth *them*; even so the Son quickeneth whom he will.

John 6:40 And this is the will of him that sent me, that every one which seeth the Son, and believeth on him, may have everlasting life: and I will raise him up at the last day.

John 6:54 Whoso eateth my flesh, and drinketh my blood, hath eternal life; and I will raise him up at the last day.

• As raising Himself from the dead.

John 2:19 Jesus answered and said unto them, Destroy this temple, and in three days I will raise it up.

John 10:18 No man taketh it from me, but I lay it down of myself. I have power to lay it down, and I have power to take it again. This commandment have I received of my Father.

• As Eternal.

Isaiah 9:6 For unto us a child is born, unto us a son is given: and the government shall be upon his shoulder: and his name shall be called Wonderful, Counsellor, The mighty God, The everlasting Father, The Prince of Peace.

Micah 5:2 But thou, Bethlehem Ephratah, *though* thou be little among the thousands of Judah, *yet* out of thee shall he come forth unto me *that is* to be ruler in Israel; whose goings forth *have been* from of old, from everlasting.

John 1:1 In the beginning was the Word, and the Word was with God, and the Word was God.

Colossians 1:17 And he is before all things, and by him all things consist.

Hebrews 1:8-10 But unto the Son *he saith*, Thy throne, O God, *is* for ever and ever: a sceptre of righteousness *is* the sceptre of thy kingdom. Thou hast loved righteousness, and hated iniquity; therefore God, *even* thy God, hath anointed thee with the oil of gladness above thy fellows. And, Thou, Lord, in the beginning hast laid the foundation of the earth; and the heavens are the works of thine hands:

Revelation 1:8 I am Alpha and Omega, the beginning and the ending, saith the Lord, which is, and which was, and which is to come, the Almighty.

- As Omnipresent.

Matthew 18:20 For where two or three are gathered together in my name, there am I in the midst of them.

Matthew 28:20 Teaching them to observe all things whatsoever I have commanded you: and, lo, I am with you always, *even* unto the end of the world. Amen.

John 3:13 And no man hath ascended up to heaven, but he that came down from heaven, *even* the Son of man which is in heaven.

- As Omnipotent.

Psalms 45:3 Gird thy sword upon *thy* thigh, O *most* mighty, with thy glory and thy majesty.

Philippians 3:21 Who shall change our vile body, that it may be fashioned like unto his glorious body, according to the working whereby he is able even to subdue all things unto himself.

Revelation 1:8 I am Alpha and Omega, the beginning and the ending, saith the Lord, which is, and which was, and which is to come, the Almighty.

- As Omniscient.

John 16:30 Now are we sure that thou knowest all things, and needest not that any man should ask thee: by this we believe that thou camest forth from God.

John 21:17 He saith unto him the third time, Simon, *son* of Jonas, lovest thou me? Peter was grieved because he said unto him the third time, Lovest thou me? And he said unto him, Lord, thou knowest all things; thou knowest that I love thee. Jesus saith unto him, Feed my sheep.

• As discerning the thoughts of the heart.

1 Kings 8:39 Then hear thou in heaven thy dwelling place, and forgive, and do, and give to every man according to his ways, whose heart thou knowest; (for thou, *even* thou only, knowest the hearts of all the children of men;)

Luke 5:22 But when Jesus perceived their thoughts, he answering said unto them, What reason ye in your hearts?

Ezekiel 11:5 And the Spirit of the LORD fell upon me, and said unto me, Speak; Thus saith the LORD; Thus have ye said, O house of Israel: for I know the things that come into your mind, *every one of* them.

John 2:24-25 But Jesus did not commit himself unto them, because he knew all *men*, And needed not that any should testify of man: for he knew what was in man.

• As unchangeable.

Malachi 3:6 For I *am* the LORD, I change not; therefore ye sons of Jacob are not consumed.

Hebrews 1:12 And as a vesture shalt thou fold them up, and they shall be changed: but thou art the same, and thy years shall not fail.

Hebrews 13:8 Jesus Christ the same yesterday, and to day, and for ever.

As having power to forgive sins.

Colossians 3:13 Forbearing one another, and forgiving one another, if any man have a quarrel against any: even as Christ forgave you, so also *do* ye.

Mark 2:7 Why doth this *man* thus speak blasphemies? who can forgive sins but God only?

Mark 2:10 But that ye may know that the Son of man hath power on earth to forgive sins, (he saith to the sick of the palsy,)

- As Giver of pastors to the Church.

Jeremiah 3:15 And I will give you pastors according to mine heart, which shall feed you with knowledge and understanding.

Ephesians 4:11-13 And he gave some, apostles; and some, prophets; and some, evangelists; and some, pastors and teachers; For the perfecting of the saints, for the work of the ministry, for the edifying of the body of Christ: Till we all come in the unity of the faith, and of the knowledge of the Son of God, unto a perfect man, unto the measure of the stature of the fullness of Christ:

- As Husband of the Church.

Isaiah 54:5 For thy Maker *is* thine husband; the LORD of hosts *is* his name; and thy Redeemer the Holy One of Israel; The God of the whole earth shall he be called.

Ephesians 5:25-32 Husbands, love your wives, even as Christ also loved the church, and gave himself for it; That he might sanctify and cleanse it with the washing of water by the word, That he might present it to himself a glorious church, not having spot, or wrinkle, or any such thing; but that it should be holy and without blemish. So ought men to love their wives as their own bodies. He that loveth his wife loveth himself. For no man ever yet hated his own flesh; but nourisheth and cherisheth it, even as the Lord the church: . . .

Isaiah 62:5 For *as* a young man marrieth a virgin, *so* shall thy sons marry thee: and *as* the bridegroom rejoiceth over the bride, *so* shall thy God rejoice over thee.

Revelation 21:2 And I John saw the holy city, new Jerusalem, coming down from God out of heaven, prepared as a bride adorned for her husband.

Revelation 21:9 And there came unto me one of the seven angels which had the seven vials full of the seven last plagues, and talked with me, saying, Come hither, I will shew thee the bride, the Lamb's wife.

- As the object of divine worship.

Acts 7:59 And they stoned Stephen, calling upon *God*, and saying, Lord Jesus, receive my spirit.

2 Corinthians 12:8-9 For this thing I besought the Lord thrice, that it might depart from me. And he said unto me, My grace is sufficient for thee: for my strength is made perfect in weakness. Most gladly therefore will I rather glory in my infirmities, that the power of Christ may rest upon me.

- As the object of faith.

Psalms 2:12 Kiss the Son, lest he be angry, and ye perish *from* the way, when his wrath is kindled but a little. Blessed *are* all they that put their trust in him.

1 Peter 2:6 Wherefore also it is contained in the scripture, Behold, I lay in Sion a chief corner stone, elect, precious: and he that believeth on him shall not be confounded.

Jeremiah 17:5 Thus saith the LORD; Cursed *be* the man that trusteth in man, and maketh flesh his arm, and whose heart departeth from the LORD.

Jeremiah 17:7 Blessed *is* the man that trusteth in the LORD, and whose hope the LORD is.

- As God, He redeems and purifies the Church to Himself.

Revelation 5:9 And they sung a new song, saying, Thou art worthy to take the book, and to open the seals thereof: for thou wast slain, and hast redeemed us to God by thy blood out of every kindred, and tongue, and people, and nation;

Titus 2:14 Who gave himself for us, that he might redeem us from all iniquity, and purify unto himself a peculiar people, zealous of good works.

- As God, He presents the Church to Himself.

Ephesians 5:27 That he might present it to himself a glorious church, not having spot, or wrinkle, or any such thing; but that it should be holy and without blemish.

Jude 1:24-25 Now unto him that is able to keep you from falling, and to present *you* faultless before the presence of his glory with exceeding joy, To the only wise God our Saviour, *be* glory and majesty, dominion and power, both now and ever. Amen.

- Saints live to Him as God.

Romans 6:11 Likewise reckon ye also yourselves to be dead indeed unto sin, but alive unto God through Jesus Christ our Lord.

Galatians 2:19 For I through the law am dead to the law, that I might live unto God.

2 Corinthians 5:15 And *that* he died for all, that they which live should not henceforth live unto themselves, but unto him which died for them, and rose again.

- Acknowledged by His Apostles.

John 20:28 And Thomas answered and said unto him, My Lord and my God.

- Acknowledged by the Old Testament saints.

Genesis 17:1 And when Abram was ninety years old and nine, the LORD appeared to Abram, and said unto him, I *am* the Almighty God; walk before me, and be thou perfect.

Genesis 48:15 And he blessed Joseph, and said, God, before whom my fathers Abraham and Isaac did walk, the God which fed me all my life long unto this day,

Genesis 32:24-30 And Jacob was left alone; and there wrestled a man with him until the breaking of the day. And when he saw that he prevailed not against him, he touched the hollow of his thigh; and the hollow of Jacob's thigh was out of joint, as he wrestled with him. And he said, Let me go, for the day breaketh. And he said, I will not let thee go, except thou bless me. And he said unto him, What *is* thy name? And he said, Jacob. And he said, Thy name shall be called no more Jacob, but Israel: for as a prince hast thou power with God and with men, and hast prevailed . . . .

Hosea 12:3-5 He took his brother by the heel in the womb, and by his strength he had power with God: Yea, he had power over the angel, and prevailed: he wept, and made supplication unto him: he found him *in* Bethel, and there he spake with us; Even the LORD God of hosts; the LORD *is* his memorial.

Judges 6:22-24 And when Gideon perceived that he *was* an angel of the LORD, Gideon said, Alas, O Lord GOD! for because I have seen an angel of the LORD face to face. And the LORD said unto him, Peace *be* unto thee; fear not: thou shalt not die. Then Gideon built an altar there unto the LORD, and called it Jehovahshalom: unto this day it *is* yet in Ophrah of the Abiezrites.

Judges 13:21-22 But the angel of the LORD did no more appear to Manoah and to his wife. Then Manoah knew that he *was* an angel of the LORD. And Manoah said unto his wife, We shall surely die, because we have seen God.

This list of compiled Scriptures are taken from the volume entitled *New Topical Textbook*, edited by R. A. Torrey and that was published 1897. As one can notice, the Lord Jesus Christ has the title of Jehovah, God our Creator and He is above all power.

There is Only One God as Scriptures teach us and as the LORD Jesus Christ confirms. There is only one way to get to heaven as the Lord Jesus Christ teaches us:

Jesus answered, "I am the way and the truth and the life. No one comes to the Father except through me. If you really knew me, you would know[b] my Father as well. From now on, you do know him and have seen him." [John 14:16].

In His conversation with Philip, the Lord confirms that he who sees Him as seen the Father. Also Thomas called the Lord My Lord and My God.

Jesus the Way to the Father

[5]And Lord replied that he is the Way:

[6]Jesus answered, "I am the way and the truth and the life. No one comes to the Father except through me. [7]If you really knew me, you would know[b] my Father as well. From now on, you do know him and have seen him."

[8]Philip said, "Lord, show us the Father and that will be enough for us" [John 14:6—8].

Furthermore, an important factor to consider in the discussion about Christ's Deity is that the LORD Jesus Christ was worshipped during His earthly ministry as we read in the following passages from the Scriptures, the inspired word of God:

- "... (the wise men) saw the young child (newborn Jesus) with Mary His mother, and fell down, and worshipped Him (JESUS—not His mother!) . . ." [Matthew 2:11].
- "And, behold, there came a leper *and worshipped Him . . ."* *[Matthew 8:2].*
- *"Then they that were in the ship came and worshipped Him, saying, 'It is true You are the Son of God'" [Matthew 14:33].*
- *"And as they went to tell His disciples, behold, Jesus met them, saying, 'All hail.' And they came and held Him by the feet, and worshipped Him"* [Matthew 28:9].
- "And when they saw Him (JESUS), they *worshipped Him;* but some doubted." [Matthew 28:17].
- "But when he saw Jesus afar off, he ran and worshipped Him." [Mark 5:6
- "And it came to pass, while He blessed them, He was parted from them, and carried up into heaven, and they worshipped Him, and returned to Jerusalem with great joy . . ." [Luke 24:52].
- "And he (a 'sinner') said, 'Lord, I believe,' and he worshipped Him." [John 9:38].
- "And again, when (The Father) brings in the First-begotten into the world, He says, 'And let all the angels of God *worship Him* (LORD Jesus Christ) [Psalm 148:2;'" [Hebrews 1:6]

10. "And I beheld, and I heard the voice of many angels round about the throne and the beasts and the elders: and the number of them was ten thousand times ten thousand, and thousands of thousands; Saying with a loud voice, 'Worthy is the Lamb (LORD Jesus Christ) that was slain to receive power, and riches, and wisdom, and strength, and honour, and glory, and blessing, And every creature which is in heaven, and on the earth, and under the earth, and such as are in the sea, and all that are in them, heard, I saying, 'Blessing, and honour, and glory, and power, be unto Him that sits on the throne, and unto the Lamb (JESUS) forever and ever. And the four beasts said, 'Amen.' And the four and twenty elders fell down and *worshipped Him* that lives forever and ever." [Revelation 5:12-14].

The worship of the LORD Jesus Christ in the Scriptures is a fact that one cannot deny. The Lord *Jesus Christ is worshipped, no one can't deny the fact.*

Keeping the worshiping issue in mind, let us remember that God says that He will not share His glory with "another." Thus, because God is sharing His glory with the LORD Jesus Christ, God is the Lord Jesus Christ.

As we can notice, the Lord Jesus Christ accepted to be worshipped as Scriptures attest; and we are also to remember that worship is only reserved to God! Based on these scenarios, one will be right to state that because the Lord Jesus Christ accepted to be worshipped, the Lord Jesus Christ is God, our Creator. He is Jehovah.

Conclusion

The Lord Jesus Christ is God, our Creator as Scriptures teach us. There is Only one God, He came to earth to save us. His name is the Lord Jesus Christ, Immanuel, God with us [Matthew 1:23. He came to save.

She will give birth to a son, and you are to give him the name Jesus,[c] because he will save his people from their sins" [Matthew 1:21]

We all need to believe in our Creator and said like Thomas said to the Lord, "My Lord and my God." This powerful statement is found in Scriptures: Thomas said to him, "My Lord and my God!" [John 20:28].

Activities for this Chapter.

1. Why do you think Scriptures teach that there is Only One God?

_____

_____

_____

_____

2. Why do you think Thomas called the Lord Jesus Christ, My Lord and My God?

_____

_____

_____

_____

3. Why do you think the Lord Jesus Christ said, "I am the Way, the Truth and Life?"

_____

_____

_____

_____

4. What do you think of the Lord's answer to Philip: "He who sees me, has seen the Father?"

_____

_____

_____

_____

5. Provide few passages from the Scriptures that show that the Lord Jesus Christ is all knowing, Omniscient.

_____

_____

_____

_____

For examples:

> [47]When Jesus saw Nathanael approaching, he said of him, "Here is a true Israelite, in whom there is nothing false."

> [48]"How do you know me?" Nathanael asked.

> Jesus answered, "I saw you while you were still under the fig tree before Philip called you."

> [49]Then Nathanael declared, "Rabbi, you are the Son of God; you are the King of Israel."

> [50]Jesus said, "You believe[k] because I told you I saw you under the fig tree. You shall see greater things than that." [51]He then added, "I tell you[l] the truth, you[m] shall see heaven open, and the angels of God ascending and descending on the Son of Man" [John 1:47-50].

Jesus Knowing their thoughts:

> Jesus knew their thoughts and said to them, "Every kingdom divided against itself will be ruined, and every city or household divided against itself will not stand [Matthew 12:25].

> [4]Knowing their thoughts, Jesus said, "Why do you entertain evil thoughts in your hearts? [Matthew 9:4].

_____

_____

_____

_____

CHAPTER 7

The Deity of the Lord Jesus Christ

In the beginning was the Word, and the Word was with God, and the Word was God. [2]He was with God in the beginning.

[3]Through him all things were made; without him nothing was made that has been made. [4]In him was life, and that life was the light of men. [5]The light shines in the darkness, but the darkness has not understood[a] it [John 1:1-5].

We started the discussion by stating that God exists and He is our Creator. Then, we elaborated the thought that we need to believe in God because without faith it is impossible to please Him as we read in Scriptures, the inspired word of God [Hebrews 11:6]. In addition, we addressed the fact that God took on Flesh and became Man as we read in Scriptures [John 1:1-14]: The Word Became Flesh:

[1] In the beginning was the Word, and the Word was with God, and the Word was God. [2] He was with God in the beginning. [3] Through him all things were made; without him nothing was made that has been made. [4] In him was life, and that life was the light of all mankind. [5] The light shines in the darkness, and the darkness has not overcome[a] it.

[6] There was a man sent from God whose name was John. [7] He came as a witness to testify concerning that light, so that through him all might believe. [8] He himself was not the light; he came only as a witness to the light.

[9] The true light that gives light to everyone was coming into the world. [10] He was in the world, and though the world was made through him, the world did not recognize him. [11] He came to that

which was his own, but his own did not receive him. [12] Yet to all who did receive him, to those who believed in his name, he gave the right to become children of God—[13] children born not of natural descent, nor of human decision or a husband's will, but born of God.

[14] The Word became flesh and made his dwelling among us. We have seen his glory, the glory of the one and only Son, who came from the Father, full of grace and truth.

Now, let us elaborate more on regarding God's nature and let us examine the reasons why God became Man. The purpose of this chapter is to elaborate more about the Deity of our Lord and Savior Jesus Christ based on Scriptures, the inspired word of God in the Holy Bible.

Scriptures teach that the Lord Jesus Christ is God, our Creator, the Creator of the universe [Genesis 1:1-31; 2:1-23; John 1:1-14; Colossians 1:1-15]. Moreover, the Lord Jesus Christ Himself teaches about creation as we read in Scriptures:

> [4] "Haven't you read," he replied, "that at the beginning the Creator 'made them male and female,'[a] [5] and said, 'For this reason a man will leave his father and mother and be united to his wife, and the two will become one flesh'[b] [Matthew 19:4-5].

Also important is that the Lord Jesus Christ teaches that there is Only One God and that He is God, Our Creator. The Lord teaches that there is Only One God: [Mark 12:29]. and He claims that He and the Father are One [John 10:30]. As I already mentioned, many passages in Scriptures teach that there is Only One God and that the LORD Jesus Christ is God, our Creator, and the Lord Jesus Christ Himself teaches that there is Only God and the Lord claims that He is God. Based on these two facts that proclaim the truth, on one hand, Scriptures, the inspired word of God, and on the other hand, the Lord Jesus Christ's claim that He is God. We will examine various passages from Scriptures as they proclaim the truth and raise challenges by teaching about the Lord Jesus Christ's Deity and we will examine the Lord's claims about Himself. Now, Is the Lord Jesus Christ, God our Creator?

The Authority and the Truth of the Scriptures, and Views on Christ's Deity.

Scriptures are the inspired word of God as we know [I Timothy 3:16] and the word of God is truth [John 17:3].Numerous passages from the Bible that teach about Christ's Deity include passages that instruct us that God Our Only Savior. For examples, the verses in the table below:

God is the only Savior.	*The Lord Jesus Christ is the Only Savior.*
"I, even I, am the LORD; and beside me there is no savior." *Isaiah 43:11*	*. . . the Father sent the Son to be the Savior of the world. 1 John 4:14*
To the only wise God our Savior . . . Jude 1:12	*. . . our Lord and Savior Jesus Christ. II Peter 3:18*
God our Savior. Titus 2:10	*. . . God and our Savior Jesus Christ. II Peter 1:1*
. . . we trust in the living God, who is the Savior. I Timothy 4:10	*. . . the Christ, the Savior of the world. John 4:42*
God my Savior. Luke 1:47	*. . . Titus 1:4*
	Luke 2:11
	—Acts 4:12
	. . .
	—2 Timothy 2:10
	. . .
	—Heb 2:10
	—Heb 5:9

God created the heavens and the earth by Himself as we read in Scriptures:

I am the LORD that maketh all things; that stretcheth forth the heavens <u>alone</u>; that spreadeth abroad the earth <u>by myself</u>. Isaiah 44:24

In the beginning God created the heaven and the earth. Genesis 1:1

God created the universe and earth by Himself.	Jesus Christ created the universe and the earth.
• Isaiah 44:24 • Genesis 1:1	• Hebrews 1:10 • Colossians 1:16 • John 1:3
God *Only God is worshipped.* • Matthew 4:10	*Jesus* *Jesus is worshipped.* • Matthew 9:18 • Hebrews 1:6 • John 20:28

It is important to read these Scriptures critically in order to get the point and analyze the messages they are transmitting.

God	*Jesus*
God created the universe and earth by Himself. *I am the LORD that maketh all things; that stretcheth forth the heavens <u>alone</u>; that spreadeth abroad the earth <u>by myself</u>. Isaiah 44:24* *In the beginning God created the heaven and the earth. Genesis 1:1*	*[U]nto the Son he saith . . . Thou, LORD, in the beginning hast laid the foundation of the earth; and the heavens are the works of thine hands. Hebrews 1:10* *[B]y him [Jesus] were all things created, that are in heaven, and that are in earth . . . all things were created by him, and for him. Colossians 1:16* *All things were made by him; and without him was not anything made that was made. John 1:3*

Other Scriptures that discuss Christ's Deity include verses that discuss God our Creator, and His nature.

Scriptures teach that God is the Word:

Scriptures teach that the Lord is Jesus Christ is the Word of God that He is The Beginning and the End. The Lord Jesus Christ is the Beginning and the End, the First and the Last in the following passages:

- *The Lord Jesus Christ is described As Jehovah, the First and the Last:*

  Revelation 22:13 I am Alpha and Omega, the beginning and the end, the first and the last.

Furthermore, the Lord Is described as Lord of All, God of all, God and Savior

- As Lord of all.

  [Acts 10:36]

  [Romans 10:11-13].

- Invoked as Jehovah.

  [Joel 2:32].

  [Acts 2:21]

  [1 Corinthians 1:2].

- As the Eternal God and Creator.

  [Psalms 102:24-27].

  [Hebrews 1:8].

  [Hebrews 1:10-12].

- As the mighty God.

  For unto us a child is born, unto us a son is given: and the government shall be upon his shoulder: and his name shall be called Wonderful, Counselor, The mighty God, The everlasting Father, The Prince of Peace [Isaiah 9:6].

- As the Great God and Savior.

  [Hosea 1:7].

  [Titus 2:13].

- As God over all.

  [Psalms 45:6-7].

- As the true God.

  [Jeremiah 10:10].

  [1 John 5:20].

- As God the Word.

  John 1:1 In the beginning was the Word, and the Word was with God, and the Word was God.

- As Emmanuel.

  [Isaiah 7:14].

  [Matthew 1:23].

All these titles are scary and they reveal who God our Creator Is, He IS the LORD Jesus Christ.

To God be the Glory!

The Lord says that He is the Way and the Truth: ⁶Jesus answered, "I am the way and *the truth* and the life. No one comes to the Father except through me [John 14:6].

He is God the Creator, as He told Philip: [John 14:1-9].

The Lord Jesus Christ is, God, our Creator as Thomas refers to Him as LORD and GOD, "My Lord and My God."

•   Jesus Appears to Thomas:

[John 19:24-30].

Even more important and worth mentioning in the discussions about the Lord Jesus Christ's Deity is that God calls the Lord Jesus, God as we read in the following passages:

[Hebrews 1:6-12].

Scriptures teach that God became Man:

[John 1-1-14].

The LORD Jesus Came to earth to save His people

He came to remove our sins:

[Matthew 1:21].

[John 1-29—34].

The Lord Jesus Christ is God because Scriptures ascribe to the LORD the Attributes which can only be referred to God. For examples. Scriptures teach us that the LORD Jesus Christ is

The Creator of the universe:

Jesus Christ is the Creator

The Bible teaches that God created everything that exists, whether spiritual or material:[Acts. 17:24].

The LORD Jesus Christ is Omnipresent

> [Matthew 18:20]

The LORD Jesus Christ is Eternal

> For unto us a child is born, . . . and his name shall be called Wonderful, Counselor, The mighty God, The everlasting Father . . . . [Isaiah 9:6]

The LORD Jesus Christ is The Judge:

> For we know Him who said, 'Vengeance is Mine, I will repay,' says the Lord. And again, 'The LORD [Jehovah] will judge His people [Hebrews 10:30].

The LORD Jesus Christ is Worshiped

> There is probably no sin more condemned in the Bible than that of idolatry. The Bible teaches that we are to worship God alone. Why?

> [Matthew 2:1-2].

The LORD Jesus Christ is the Savior, [John 14:6]:

Jesus answered, "I am the way and the truth and the life.

> Although the LORD Jesus Christ was called the Son of God, the name "Son of God" and the title as "Lord" denote His Deity.

Passages in which the Lord Jesus Christ

1. Jesus Christ the Son of God:[Matthew 26:63-65]

His Coming to earth was predicated

He was worshiped: [Philippians 2:11]

He is LORD:

In discussing the Deity of the LORD Jesus Christ, many scholars have presented tables with verses from the Scriptures from the Old Testament, side by side with Scriptures from the New Testament to help those who do not believe that the Lord Jesus Christ is God to see in a more clear way. Such example is the following table by Reverend Matt as presented on the Carm webpage the table reads: Jesus Is God, and the Scriptures stand side by side.

1.   *Table by Matt Slick:*

- Jesus is God

- *by Matt Slick*

- "You are my witnesses," declares the LORD, "and my servant whom I have chosen, so that you may know and believe me and understand that I am he. Before me no god was formed, nor will there be one after me," (Isaiah 43:10).

JESUS	**IS**	**GOD, "YAHWEH"**

John 1:3, "Through him all things were made; without him nothing was made that has been made."

Col. 1:16-17, "For by him all things were created: things in heaven and on earth, visible and invisible, whether thrones or powers or rulers or authorities; all things were created by him and for him. He is before all things, and in him all things hold together."

Creator

Job 33:4, "The Spirit of God has made me; the breath of the Almighty gives me life."

Isaiah 40:28, "Do you not know? Have you not heard? The LORD is the everlasting God, the Creator of the ends of the earth. He will not grow tired or weary, and his understanding no one can fathom."

Rev. 1:17, "When I saw him, I fell at his feet as though dead. Then he placed his right hand on me and said: 'Do not be afraid. I am the First and the Last.'"

Rev. 2:8, "To the angel of the church in Smyrna write: These are the words of him who is the First and the Last, who died and came to life again."

First and Last

Isaiah 41:4, "Who has done this and carried it through, calling forth the generations from the beginning? I, the LORD—with the first of them and with the last—I am he."

Isaiah 44:6, "This is what the LORD says—Israel's King and Redeemer, the LORD Almighty: I am the first and I am the last; apart from me there is no God."

Rev. 22:13, "I am the Alpha and the Omega, the First and the Last, the Beginning and the End."

Isaiah 48:12, "Listen to me, O Jacob, Israel, whom I have called: I am he; I am the first and I am the last."

John 8:24, "Therefore I said to you that you will die in your sins; for if you do not believe that I am He, you will die in your sins." (NKJV)

John 8:58, "I tell you the truth," Jesus answered, "before Abraham was born, I am!" See Exodus 3:14

John 13:19, "I am telling you now before it happens, so that when it does happen you will believe that I am He."

I AM

"ego eimi"

Exodus 3:14, "God said to Moses, "I AM WHO I AM. This is what you are to say to the Israelites: 'I AM has sent me to you.'"

Isaiah 43:10, "You are my witnesses," declares the LORD, "and my servant whom I have chosen, so that you may know and believe me and understand that I am he. Before me no god was formed, nor will there be one after me."

See also Deut. 32:39

Joel 3:12, "Let the nations be roused; let them advance into the Valley of Jehoshaphat, for there I will sit to judge all the nations on every side."

2 Tim. 4:1, "In the presence of God and of Christ Jesus, who will judge the living and the dead, and in view of his appearing and his kingdom, I give you this charge . . ."

2 Cor. 5:10, "For we must all appear before the judgment seat of Christ, that each one may receive what is due him for the things done while in the body, whether good or bad."

Judge

Rom. 14:10, "You, then, why do you judge your brother? Or why do you look down on your brother? For we will all stand before God's judgment seat."

Matt. 2:2, ". . . Where is the one who has been born king of the Jews? We saw his star in the east and have come to worship him."

Luke 23:3, "So Pilate asked Jesus, "Are you the king of the Jews?" "Yes, it is as you say," Jesus replied."

See also John 19:21

King

Jer. 10:10, "But the LORD is the true God; he is the living God, the eternal King. When he is angry, the earth trembles; the nations cannot endure his wrath."

Isaiah 44:6-8, "This is what the LORD says—Israel's King and Redeemer, the LORD Almighty: I am the first and I am the last; apart from me there is no God."

See also Psalm 47

Psalm 27:1, "The LORD is my light and my salvation—whom shall I fear?"

John 8:12, "When Jesus spoke again to the people, he said, "I am the light of the world. Whoever follows me will never walk in darkness, but will have the light of life."

Luke 2:32, "a light for revelation to the Gentiles and for glory to your people Israel."

See also John 1:7-9

Light

Isaiah 60:20, "our sun will never set again, and your moon will wane no more; the LORD will be your everlasting light, and your days of sorrow will end."

1 John 1:5, "God is light; in him there is no darkness at all."

1 Cor. 10:4, ". . . for they drank from the spiritual rock that accompanied them, and that rock was Christ."

See also 1 Pet. 2:4-8.

Rock

Deut. 32:4, "He is the Rock, his works are perfect, and all his ways are just. A faithful God who does no wrong, upright and just is he."

See also 2 Sam. 22:32 and Isaiah 17:10.

John 4:42, "They said to the woman, 'We no longer believe just because of what you said; now we have heard for ourselves, and we know that this man really is the Savior of the world.'"

1 John 4:14, "And we have seen and testify that the Father has sent his Son to be the Savior of the world."

Savior

Isaiah 43:3, "For I am the LORD, your God, the Holy One of Israel, your Savior"

Isaiah 45:21, ". . . And there is no God apart from me, a righteous God and a Savior; there is none but me."

John 10:11, "I am the good shepherd. The good shepherd lays down his life for the sheep."

Heb. 13:20, "May the God of peace, who through the blood of the eternal covenant brought back from the dead our Lord Jesus, that great Shepherd of the sheep,"

See also John 10:14,16; 1 Pet. 2:25

Shepherd

Psalm 23:1, "The LORD is my shepherd, I shall not be in want."

Isaiah 40:11, "He tends his flock like a shepherd: He gathers the lambs in his arms and carries them close to his heart; he gently leads those that have young."

- Unless otherwise noted, all quotations are from the NASB.

2.   The Juxtapose Scriptures about Christ's Deity from the New Topical Textbook, edited by R. A. Torrey, published 1897, which I have reported in this book is a powerful table to examine.

Statements from the Scriptures in the Holy Bible inform us that there is Only One God [Mark 12:29]; Deuteronomy 4:6].

The Lord Jesus Christ's Claim about Himself:

> Finally, Let us examine the Lord Jesus Christ's claim about Himself. Did Jesus Christ teach that He is God? Please le us read the following passages:
>
> > I and the father are One [John 10:30]
> >
> > [24] I told you that you would die in your sins; if you do not believe that I am he, you will indeed die in your sins"[John 8:24].
> >
> > "Very truly I tell you," Jesus answered, "before Abraham was born, I am!":[John 8:58]. Before Abraham was born I am

Conclusion

The LORD Jesus Christ is God, our Creator as Scriptures teach and as He teaches: [John 8:24].

Scriptures teach about Christ. A closer examination of Scriptures reveal that there is Only One God, Our Creator, the Creator of the heavens and the earth and that the Lord Jesus Christ is God, our Creator, the Creator of the heavens and the earth, the Creator of the universe.

Activities for this chapter

1. Which passage or passages the LORD has stated about Himself has or have convinced you the most about WHO HE IS?

_____

_____

_____

_____

2. When the LORD rose from the death, He showed Himself to His disciples, one of them heard about the good news, but he doubted, then, the LORD appeared in the house where the disciples were gathered and He showed Himself to them; then, the LORD asked Thomas to put his fingers into His Hands and Thomas said: "My LORD and My God." Please find the references of the event in Scriptures and write it down in to fill the following blank line:

_____

_____

_____

_____

3. What do you think of this scenario, as the Lord reveals Himself to Thomas and Thomas fell to the Lord's feet?

_____

_____

_____

_____

CHAPTER 8

Lord Jesus Christ, the Alpha and the Omega

"I am the Alpha and the Omega," says the Lord God, "who is, and who was, and who is to come, the Almighty" [Revelation 1:8].

Passages from the Old Testament

Passages from the New Testament

Rev. 1:17, "When I saw him, I fell at his feet as though dead. Then he placed his right hand on me and said: 'Do not be afraid. I am the First and the Last.'" Rev. 1:17,

Isaiah 41:4, "Who has done this and carried it through, calling forth the generations from the beginning? I, the LORD—with the first of them and with the last—I am he."

Rev. 2:8, "To the angel of the church in Smyrna write: These are the words of him who is the First and the Last, who died and came to life again."

First and Last

Isaiah 44:6, "This is what the LORD says—Israel's King and Redeemer, the LORD Almighty: I am the first and I am the last; apart from me there is no God."

Rev. 22:13, "I am the Alpha and the Omega, the First and the Last, the Beginning and the End."

Isaiah 48:12, "Listen to me, O Jacob, Israel, whom I have called: I am he; I am the first and I am the last."

The First and the Last

God is the First and the Last and it is written about the Lord Jesus Christ that He is the First and the Last. 2 passages deserve to be mentioned here, one is from the Book of Genesis and the second comes from the book of John.

In the Book of Genesis we read that in the beginning God created the heavens and the earth and every creatures [Genesis 1:1-29]. Moreover, in the Book of Revelation, we read that the Lord Jesus Christ is The Beginning and the End [Revelation 1:8]. In addition, the book of John informs us about the beginning, in the beginning was the Word and the word was with God and the Word was God and the Word became Flesh [John 1:1-14].

Other passages from the Holy Bible that show that the Lord Jesus Christ is God include the following:

- [15]The Son is the image of the invisible God, the firstborn over all creation. [16] For in him all things were created: things in heaven and on earth, visible and invisible, whether thrones or powers or rulers or authorities; all things have been created through him and for him. [17] He is before all things, and in him all things hold together. [18] And he is the head of the body, the church; he is the beginning and the firstborn from among the dead, so that in everything he might have the supremacy. [19] For God was pleased to have all his fullness dwell in him, [20] and through him to reconcile to himself all things, whether things on earth or things in heaven, by making peace through his blood, shed on the cross [Colossians 1:15].

- The Word Became Flesh

  [1] In the beginning was the Word, and the Word was with God, and the Word was God. [2] He was with God in the beginning. [3] Through him all things were made; without him nothing was made that has been made. [4] In him was life, and that life was the light of all mankind. [5] The light shines in the darkness, and the darkness has not overcome[a] it.

  [6] There was a man sent from God whose name was John. [7] He came as a witness to testify concerning that light, so that through him all might believe. [8] He himself was not the light; he came only as a witness to the light.

⁹ The true light that gives light to everyone was coming into the world. ¹⁰ He was in the world, and though the world was made through him, the world did not recognize him. ¹¹ He came to that which was his own, but his own did not receive him. ¹² Yet to all who did receive him, to those who believed in his name, he gave the right to become children of God—¹³ children born not of natural descent, nor of human decision or a husband's will, but born of God.

¹⁴ The Word became flesh and made his dwelling among us. We have seen his glory, the glory of the one and only Son, who came from the Father, full of grace and truth [John 1:1-14].

The Lord Jesus Christ is God because Scriptures describe Him with the titles that Only God has. Among these titles are the description of Christ as Jehovah, the Shepherd and the Creator. Christ is described with the following powerful tiles: titles:

- As Jehovah.

  Isaiah 40:3 The voice of him that crieth in the wilderness, Prepare ye the way of the LORD, make straight in the desert a highway for our God.

  Matthew 3:3 For this is he that was spoken of by the prophet Esaias, saying, The voice of one crying in the wilderness, Prepare ye the way of the Lord, make his paths straight.

- As Jehovah of glory.

  Psalms 24:7 Lift up your heads, O ye gates; and be ye lift up, ye everlasting doors; and the King of glory shall come in.

  Psalms 24:10 Who is this King of glory? The LORD of hosts, he *is* the King of glory. Selah.

  1 Corinthians 2:8 Which none of the princes of this world knew: for had they known *it*, they would not have crucified the Lord of glory.

James 2:1 My brethren, have not the faith of our Lord Jesus Christ, *the Lord* of glory, with respect of persons.

- As Jehovah, our RIGHTEOUSNESS.

Jeremiah 23:5-6 Behold, the days come, saith the LORD, that I will raise unto David a righteous Branch, and a King shall reign and prosper, and shall execute judgment and justice in the earth. In his days Judah shall be saved, and Israel shall dwell safely: and this *is* his name whereby he shall be called, THE LORD OUR RIGHTEOUSNESS.

1 Corinthians 1:30 But of him are ye in Christ Jesus, who of God is made unto us wisdom, and righteousness, and sanctification, and redemption:

- As Jehovah, above all.

Psalms 97:9 For thou, LORD, *art* high above all the earth: thou art exalted far above all gods.

John 3:31 He that cometh from above is above all: he that is of the earth is earthly, and speaketh of the earth: he that cometh from heaven is above all.

- As Jehovah, the First and the Last.

Isaiah 44:6 Thus saith the LORD the King of Israel, and his redeemer the LORD of hosts; I *am* the first, and I *am* the last; and beside me *there is* no God.

Revelation 1:17 And when I saw him, I fell at his feet as dead. And he laid his right hand upon me, saying unto me, Fear not; I am the first and the last:

Isaiah 48:12-16 Hearken unto me, O Jacob and Israel, my called; I *am* he; I *am* the first, I also *am* the last. Mine hand also hath laid the foundation of the earth, and my right hand hath spanned the

heavens: *when* I call unto them, they stand up together. All ye, assemble yourselves, and hear; which among them hath declared these *things*? The LORD hath loved him: he will do his pleasure on Babylon, and his arm *shall be on* the Chaldeans. I, *even* I, have spoken; yea, I have called him: I have brought him, and he shall make his way prosperous. Come ye near unto me, hear ye this; I have not spoken in secret from the beginning; from the time that it was, there *am* I: and now the Lord GOD, and his Spirit, hath sent me . . . .

Revelation 22:13 I am Alpha and Omega, the beginning and the end, the first and the last.

- As Jehovah's Fellow and Equal.

Zechariah 13:7 Awake, O sword, against my shepherd, and against the man *that is* my fellow, saith the LORD of hosts: smite the shepherd, and the sheep shall be scattered: and I will turn mine hand upon the little ones.

Philippians 2:6 Who, being in the form of God, thought it not robbery to be equal with God:

- As Jehovah of Hosts.

Isaiah 6:1-3 In the year that king Uzziah died I saw also the Lord sitting upon a throne, high and lifted up, and his train filled the temple. Above it stood the seraphims: each one had six wings; with twain he covered his face, and with twain he covered his feet, and with twain he did fly. And one cried unto another, and said, Holy, holy, holy, *is* the LORD of hosts: the whole earth *is* full of his glory.

John 12:41 These things said Esaias, when he saw his glory, and spake of him.

Isaiah 8:13-14 Sanctify the LORD of hosts himself; and *let* him *be* your fear, and *let* him *be* your dread. And he shall be for a

sanctuary; but for a stone of stumbling and for a rock of offence to both the houses of Israel, for a gin and for a snare to the inhabitants of Jerusalem.

1 Peter 2:8 And a stone of stumbling, and a rock of offence, *even to them* which stumble at the word, being disobedient: whereunto also they were appointed.

• As Jehovah, the Shepherd.

Isaiah 40:11 He shall feed his flock like a shepherd: he shall gather the lambs with his arm, and carry *them* in his bosom, *and* shall gently lead those that are with young.

Hebrews 13:20 Now the God of peace, that brought again from the dead our Lord Jesus, that great shepherd of the sheep, through the blood of the everlasting covenant,

• As Jehovah, for whose glory all things were created.

Proverbs 16:4 The LORD hath made all *things* for himself: yea, even the wicked for the day of evil.

Colossians 1:16 For by him were all things created, that are in heaven, and that are in earth, visible and invisible, whether *they be* thrones, or dominions, or principalities, or powers: all things were created by him, and for him:

• As Jehovah, the Messenger of the covenant.

Malachi 3:1 Behold, I will send my messenger, and he shall prepare the way before me: and the Lord, whom ye seek, shall suddenly come to his temple, even the messenger of the covenant, whom ye delight in: behold, he shall come, saith the LORD of hosts.

Mark 1:2 As it is written in the prophets, Behold, I send my messenger before thy face, which shall prepare thy way before thee.

Luke 2:27 And he came by the Spirit into the temple: and when the parents brought in the child Jesus, to do for him after the custom of the law,

- Invoked as Jehovah.

Joel 2:32 And it shall come to pass, *that* whosoever shall call on the name of the LORD shall be delivered: for in mount Zion and in Jerusalem shall be deliverance, as the LORD hath said, and in the remnant whom the LORD shall call.

Acts 2:21 And it shall come to pass, *that* whosoever shall call on the name of the Lord shall be saved.

1 Corinthians 1:2 Unto the church of God which is at Corinth, to them that are sanctified in Christ Jesus, called *to be* saints, with all that in every place call upon the name of Jesus Christ our Lord, both theirs and ours:

- As the Eternal God and Creator.

Psalms 102:24-27 I said, O my God, take me not away in the midst of my days: thy years *are* throughout all generations. Of old hast thou laid the foundation of the earth: and the heavens *are* the work of thy hands. They shall perish, but thou shalt endure: yea, all of them shall wax old like a garment; as a vesture shalt thou change them, and they shall be changed: But thou *art* the same, and thy years shall have no end.

Hebrews 1:8 But unto the Son *he saith*, Thy throne, O God, *is* for ever and ever: a sceptre of righteousness *is* the sceptre of thy kingdom.

Hebrews 1:10-12 And, Thou, Lord, in the beginning hast laid the foundation of the earth; and the heavens are the works of thine hands: They shall perish; but thou remainest; and they all shall wax old as doth a garment; And as a vesture shalt thou fold them

up, and they shall be changed: but thou art the same, and thy
years shall not fail.

- As the mighty God.

Isaiah 9:6 For unto us a child is born, unto us a son is given: and
the government shall be upon his shoulder: and his name shall be
called Wonderful, Counsellor, The mighty God, The everlasting
Father, The Prince of Peace.

- As the Great God and Saviour.

Hosea 1:7 But I will have mercy upon the house of Judah, and
will save them by the LORD their God, and will not save them by
bow, nor by sword, nor by battle, by horses, nor by horsemen.

Titus 2:13 Looking for that blessed hope, and the glorious
appearing of the great God and our Saviour Jesus Christ;

- As God over all.

Psalms 45:6-7 Thy throne, O God, *is* for ever and ever: the sceptre
of thy kingdom *is* a right sceptre. Thou lovest righteousness, and
hatest wickedness: therefore God, thy God, hath anointed thee
with the oil of gladness above thy fellows.

- As the true God.

Jeremiah 10:10 But the LORD *is* the true God, he *is* the living
God, and an everlasting king: at his wrath the earth shall tremble,
and the nations shall not be able to abide his indignation.

1 John 5:20 And we know that the Son of God is come, and hath
given us an understanding, that we may know him that is true,
and we are in him that is true, *even* in his Son Jesus Christ. This is
the true God, and eternal life.

- As God the Word.

  John 1:1 In the beginning was the Word, and the Word was with God, and the Word was God.

- As God, the Judge.

  Ecclesiastes 12:14 For God shall bring every work into judgment, with every secret thing, whether *it be* good, or whether *it be* evil.

  1 Corinthians 4:5 Therefore judge nothing before the time, until the Lord come, who both will bring to light the hidden things of darkness, and will make manifest the counsels of the hearts: and then shall every man have praise of God.

  2 Corinthians 5:10 For we must all appear before the judgment seat of Christ; that every one may receive the things *done* in *his* body, according to that he hath done, whether *it be* good or bad.

  2 Timothy 4:1 I charge *thee* therefore before God, and the Lord Jesus Christ, who shall judge the quick and the dead at his appearing and his kingdom;

- As Emmanuel.

  Isaiah 7:14 Therefore the Lord himself shall give you a sign; Behold, a virgin shall conceive, and bear a son, and shall call his name Immanuel.

  Matthew 1:23 Behold, a virgin shall be with child, and shall bring forth a son, and they shall call his name Emmanuel, which being interpreted is, God with us.

- As King of kings and Lord of lords.

  Daniel 10:17 For how can the servant of this my lord talk with this my lord? for as for me, straightway there remained no strength in me, neither is there breath left in me.

Revelation 1:5 And from Jesus Christ, *who is* the faithful witness, *and* the first begotten of the dead, and the prince of the kings of the earth. Unto him that loved us, and washed us from our sins in his own blood,

Revelation 17:14 These shall make war with the Lamb, and the Lamb shall overcome them: for he is Lord of lords, and King of kings: and they that are with him *are* called, and chosen, and faithful.

- As the Holy One.

  1 Samuel 2:2 *There is* none holy as the LORD: for *there is* none beside thee: neither *is there* any rock like our God.

  Acts 3:14 But ye denied the Holy One and the Just, and desired a murderer to be granted unto you;

- As the Lord from heaven.

  1 Corinthians 15:47 The first man *is* of the earth, earthy: the second man *is* the Lord from heaven.

- As Lord of the sabbath.

  Genesis 2:3 And God blessed the seventh day, and sanctified it: because that in it he had rested from all his work which God created and made.

  Matthew 12:8 For the Son of man is Lord even of the sabbath day.

- As Lord of all.

  Acts 10:36 The word which *God* sent unto the children of Israel, preaching peace by Jesus Christ: (he is Lord of all:)

  Romans 10:11-13 For the scripture saith, Whosoever believeth on him shall not be ashamed. For there is no difference between the Jew and the Greek: for the same Lord over all is rich unto all that call upon him. For whosoever shall call upon the name of the Lord shall be saved.

- As Son of God.

Matthew 26:63-67 But Jesus held his peace. And the high priest answered and said unto him, I adjure thee by the living God, that thou tell us whether thou be the Christ, the Son of God. Jesus saith unto him, Thou hast said: nevertheless I say unto you, Hereafter shall ye see the Son of man sitting on the right hand of power, and coming in the clouds of heaven. Then the high priest rent his clothes, saying, He hath spoken blasphemy; what further need have we of witnesses? behold, now ye have heard his blasphemy. What think ye? They answered and said, He is guilty of death. Then did they spit in his face, and buffeted him; and others smote *him* with the palms of their hands, . . .

- As the Only-begotten Son of the Father.

John 1:14 And the Word was made flesh, and dwelt among us, (and we beheld his glory, the glory as of the only begotten of the Father,) full of grace and truth.

John 3:16 For God so loved the world, that he gave his only begotten Son, that whosoever believeth in him should not perish, but have everlasting life.

John 3:18 He that believeth on him is not condemned: but he that believeth not is condemned already, because he hath not believed in the name of the only begotten Son of God.

1 John 4:9 In this was manifested the love of God toward us, because that God sent his only begotten Son into the world, that we might live through him.

• His blood is called the blood of God.

Acts 20:28 Take heed therefore unto yourselves, and to all the flock, over the which the Holy Ghost hath made you overseers, to feed the church of God, which he hath purchased with his own blood.

• As one with the Father.

John 10:30 I and *my* Father are one.

John 12:45 And he that seeth me seeth him that sent me.

John 14:7-10 If ye had known me, ye should have known my Father also: and from henceforth ye know him, and have seen him. Philip saith unto him, Lord, shew us the Father, and it sufficeth us. Jesus saith unto him, Have I been so long time with you, and yet hast thou not known me, Philip? he that hath seen me hath seen the Father; and how sayest thou *then*, Shew us the Father? Believest thou not that I am in the Father, and the Father in me? the words that I speak unto you I speak not of myself: but the Father that dwelleth in me, he doeth the works.

John 17:10 And all mine are thine, and thine are mine; and I am glorified in them.

• As sending the Spirit, equally with the Father.

John 14:16 And I will pray the Father, and he shall give you another Comforter, that he may abide with you for ever;

John 15:26 But when the Comforter is come, whom I will send unto you from the Father, *even* the Spirit of truth, which proceedeth from the Father, he shall testify of me:

- As entitled to equal honor with the Father.

John 5:23 That all *men* should honour the Son, even as they honour the Father. He that honoureth not the Son honoureth not the Father which hath sent him.

- As Owner of all things, equally with the Father.

John 16:15 All things that the Father hath are mine: therefore said I, that he shall take of mine, and shall shew *it* unto you.

- As unrestricted by the law of the sabbath, equally with the Father.

John 5:17 But Jesus answered them, My Father worketh hitherto, and I work.

- As the Source of grace, equally with the Father.

1 Thessalonians 3:11 Now God himself and our Father, and our Lord Jesus Christ, direct our way unto you.

2 Thessalonians 2:16-17 Now our Lord Jesus Christ himself, and God, even our Father, which hath loved us, and hath given *us* everlasting consolation and good hope through grace, Comfort your hearts, and stablish you in every good word and work.

- As unsearchable, equally with the Father.

Proverbs 30:4 Who hath ascended up into heaven, or descended? who hath gathered the wind in his fists? who hath bound the waters in a garment? who hath established all the ends of the earth? what *is* his name, and what *is* his son's name, if thou canst tell?

Matthew 11:27 All things are delivered unto me of my Father: and no man knoweth the Son, but the Father; neither knoweth any man the Father, save the Son, and *he* to whomsoever the Son will reveal *him*.

- As Creator of all things.

  Isaiah 40:28 Hast thou not known? hast thou not heard, *that* the everlasting God, the LORD, the Creator of the ends of the earth, fainteth not, neither is weary? *there is* no searching of his understanding.

  John 1:3 All things were made by him; and without him was not any thing made that was made.

  Colossians 1:16 For by him were all things created, that are in heaven, and that are in earth, visible and invisible, whether *they be* thrones, or dominions, or principalities, or powers: all things were created by him, and for him:

  Hebrews 1:2 Hath in these last days spoken unto us by *his* Son, whom he hath appointed heir of all things, by whom also he made the worlds;

- As Supporter and Preserver of all things.

  Nehemiah 9:6 Thou, *even* thou, *art* LORD alone; thou hast made heaven, the heaven of heavens, with all their host, the earth, and all *things* that *are* therein, the seas, and all that *is* therein, and thou preservest them all; and the host of heaven worshippeth thee.

  Colossians 1:17 And he is before all things, and by him all things consist.

  Hebrews 1:3 Who being the brightness of *his* glory, and the express image of his person, and upholding all things by the word of his power, when he had by himself purged our sins, sat down on the right hand of the Majesty on high;

- As possessed of the fulness of the God head.

  Colossians 2:9 For in him dwelleth all the fulness of the Godhead bodily.

  Hebrews 1:3 Who being the brightness of *his* glory, and the express image of his person, and upholding all things by the word of his power, when he had by himself purged our sins, sat down on the right hand of the Majesty on high;

- As raising the dead.

  John 5:21 For as the Father raiseth up the dead, and quickeneth *them*; even so the Son quickeneth whom he will.

  John 6:40 And this is the will of him that sent me, that every one which seeth the Son, and believeth on him, may have everlasting life: and I will raise him up at the last day.

  John 6:54 Whoso eateth my flesh, and drinketh my blood, hath eternal life; and I will raise him up at the last day.

- As raising Himself from the dead.

  John 2:19 Jesus answered and said unto them, Destroy this temple, and in three days I will raise it up.

  John 10:18 No man taketh it from me, but I lay it down of myself. I have power to lay it down, and I have power to take it again. This commandment have I received of my Father.

- As Eternal.

  Isaiah 9:6 For unto us a child is born, unto us a son is given: and the government shall be upon his shoulder: and his name shall be called Wonderful, Counsellor, The mighty God, The everlasting Father, The Prince of Peace.

Micah 5:2 But thou, Bethlehem Ephratah, *though* thou be little among the thousands of Judah, *yet* out of thee shall he come forth unto me *that is* to be ruler in Israel; whose goings forth *have been* from of old, from everlasting.

John 1:1 In the beginning was the Word, and the Word was with God, and the Word was God.

Colossians 1:17 And he is before all things, and by him all things consist.

Hebrews 1:8-10 But unto the Son *he saith*, Thy throne, O God, *is* for ever and ever: a sceptre of righteousness *is* the sceptre of thy kingdom. Thou hast loved righteousness, and hated iniquity; therefore God, *even* thy God, hath anointed thee with the oil of gladness above thy fellows. And, Thou, Lord, in the beginning hast laid the foundation of the earth; and the heavens are the works of thine hands:

Revelation 1:8 I am Alpha and Omega, the beginning and the ending, saith the Lord, which is, and which was, and which is to come, the Almighty.

- As Omnipresent.

Matthew 18:20 For where two or three are gathered together in my name, there am I in the midst of them.

Matthew 28:20 Teaching them to observe all things whatsoever I have commanded you: and, lo, I am with you alway, *even* unto the end of the world. Amen.

John 3:13 And no man hath ascended up to heaven, but he that came down from heaven, *even* the Son of man which is in heaven.

- As Omnipotent.

Psalms 45:3 Gird thy sword upon *thy* thigh, O *most* mighty, with thy glory and thy majesty.

Philippians 3:21 Who shall change our vile body, that it may be fashioned like unto his glorious body, according to the working whereby he is able even to subdue all things unto himself.

Revelation 1:8 I am Alpha and Omega, the beginning and the ending, saith the Lord, which is, and which was, and which is to come, the Almighty.

- As Omniscient.

John 16:30 Now are we sure that thou knowest all things, and needest not that any man should ask thee: by this we believe that thou camest forth from God.

John 21:17 He saith unto him the third time, Simon, *son* of Jonas, lovest thou me? Peter was grieved because he said unto him the third time, Lovest thou me? And he said unto him, Lord, thou knowest all things; thou knowest that I love thee. Jesus saith unto him, Feed my sheep.

- As discerning the thoughts of the heart.

1 Kings 8:39 Then hear thou in heaven thy dwelling place, and forgive, and do, and give to every man according to his ways, whose heart thou knowest; (for thou, *even* thou only, knowest the hearts of all the children of men;)
Luke 5:22 But when Jesus perceived their thoughts, he answering said unto them, What reason ye in your hearts?

Ezekiel 11:5 And the Spirit of the LORD fell upon me, and said unto me, Speak; Thus saith the LORD; Thus have ye said, O house of Israel: for I know the things that come into your mind, *every one of* them.

John 2:24-25 But Jesus did not commit himself unto them, because he knew all *men*, And needed not that any should testify of man: for he knew what was in man.

- As unchangeable.

Malachi 3:6 For I *am* the LORD, I change not; therefore ye sons of Jacob are not consumed.

Hebrews 1:12 And as a vesture shalt thou fold them up, and they shall be changed: but thou art the same, and thy years shall not fail.

Hebrews 13:8 Jesus Christ the same yesterday, and to day, and for ever.

As having power to forgive sins.

Colossians 3:13 Forbearing one another, and forgiving one another, if any man have a quarrel against any: even as Christ forgave you, so also *do* ye.

Mark 2:7 Why doth this *man* thus speak blasphemies? who can forgive sins but God only?

Mark 2:10 But that ye may know that the Son of man hath power on earth to forgive sins, (he saith to the sick of the palsy,)

- As Giver of pastors to the Church.

Jeremiah 3:15 And I will give you pastors according to mine heart, which shall feed you with knowledge and understanding.

Ephesians 4:11-13 And he gave some, apostles; and some, prophets; and some, evangelists; and some, pastors and teachers; For the perfecting of the saints, for the work of the ministry, for the edifying of the body of Christ: Till we all come in the unity of the faith, and of the knowledge of the Son of God, unto a perfect man, unto the measure of the stature of the fulness of Christ:

- As Husband of the Church.

Isaiah 54:5 For thy Maker *is* thine husband; the LORD of hosts *is* his name; and thy Redeemer the Holy One of Israel; The God of the whole earth shall he be called.

Ephesians 5:25-32 Husbands, love your wives, even as Christ also loved the church, and gave himself for it; That he might sanctify and cleanse it with the washing of water by the word, That he might present it to himself a glorious church, not having spot, or wrinkle, or any such thing; but that it should be holy and without blemish. So ought men to love their wives as their own bodies. He that loveth his wife loveth himself. For no man ever yet hated his own flesh; but nourisheth and cherisheth it, even as the Lord the church: . . .

Isaiah 62:5 For *as* a young man marrieth a virgin, *so* shall thy sons marry thee: and *as* the bridegroom rejoiceth over the bride, *so* shall thy God rejoice over thee.

Revelation 21:2 And I John saw the holy city, new Jerusalem, coming down from God out of heaven, prepared as a bride adorned for her husband.

Revelation 21:9 And there came unto me one of the seven angels which had the seven vials full of the seven last plagues, and talked with me, saying, Come hither, I will shew thee the bride, the Lamb's wife.

- As the object of divine worship.

Acts 7:59 And they stoned Stephen, calling upon *God*, and saying, Lord Jesus, receive my spirit.

2 Corinthians 12:8-9 For this thing I besought the Lord thrice, that it might depart from me. And he said unto me, My grace is sufficient for thee: for my strength is made perfect in weakness. Most gladly therefore will I rather glory in my infirmities, that the power of Christ may rest upon me.

- As the object of faith.

Psalms 2:12 Kiss the Son, lest he be angry, and ye perish *from* the way, when his wrath is kindled but a little. Blessed *are* all they that put their trust in him.

1 Peter 2:6 Wherefore also it is contained in the scripture, Behold, I lay in Sion a chief corner stone, elect, precious: and he that believeth on him shall not be confounded.

Jeremiah 17:5 Thus saith the LORD; Cursed *be* the man that trusteth in man, and maketh flesh his arm, and whose heart departeth from the LORD.

Jeremiah 17:7 Blessed *is* the man that trusteth in the LORD, and whose hope the LORD is.

- As God, He redeems and purifies the Church to Himself.

Revelation 5:9 And they sung a new song, saying, Thou art worthy to take the book, and to open the seals thereof: for thou wast slain, and hast redeemed us to God by thy blood out of every kindred, and tongue, and people, and nation;

Titus 2:14 Who gave himself for us, that he might redeem us from all iniquity, and purify unto himself a peculiar people, zealous of good works.

- As God, He presents the Church to Himself.

Ephesians 5:27 That he might present it to himself a glorious church, not having spot, or wrinkle, or any such thing; but that it should be holy and without blemish.

Jude 1:24-25 Now unto him that is able to keep you from falling, and to present *you* faultless before the presence of his glory with exceeding joy, To the only wise God our Saviour, *be* glory and majesty, dominion and power, both now and ever. Amen.

- Saints live to Him as God.

Romans 6:11 Likewise reckon ye also yourselves to be dead indeed unto sin, but alive unto God through Jesus Christ our Lord.

Galatians 2:19 For I through the law am dead to the law, that I might live unto God.

2 Corinthians 5:15 And *that* he died for all, that they which live should not henceforth live unto themselves, but unto him which died for them, and rose again.

- Acknowledged by His Apostles.

John 20:28 And Thomas answered and said unto him, My Lord and my God.

- Acknowledged by the Old Testament saints.

Genesis 17:1 And when Abram was ninety years old and nine, the LORD appeared to Abram, and said unto him, I *am* the Almighty God; walk before me, and be thou perfect.

Genesis 48:15 And he blessed Joseph, and said, God, before whom my fathers Abraham and Isaac did walk, the God which fed me all my life long unto this day,

Genesis 32:24-30 And Jacob was left alone; and there wrestled a man with him until the breaking of the day. And when he saw that he prevailed not against him, he touched the hollow of his thigh; and the hollow of Jacob's thigh was out of joint, as he wrestled with him. And he said, Let me go, for the day breaketh. And he said, I will not let thee go, except thou bless me. And he said unto him, What *is* thy name? And he said, Jacob. And he said, Thy name shall be called no more Jacob, but Israel: for as a prince hast thou power with God and with men, and hast prevailed . . . .

Hosea 12:3-5 He took his brother by the heel in the womb, and by his strength he had power with God: Yea, he had power over the angel, and prevailed: he wept, and made supplication unto him: he found him *in* Bethel, and there he spake with us; Even the LORD God of hosts; the LORD *is* his memorial.

Judges 6:22-24 And when Gideon perceived that he *was* an angel of the LORD, Gideon said, Alas, O Lord GOD! for because I have seen an angel of the LORD face to face. And the LORD said unto him, Peace *be* unto thee; fear not: thou shalt not die. Then Gideon built an altar there unto the LORD, and called it Jehovahshalom: unto this day it *is* yet in Ophrah of the Abiezrites.

Judges 13:21-22 But the angel of the LORD did no more appear to Manoah and to his wife. Then Manoah knew that he *was* an angel of the LORD. And Manoah said unto his wife, We shall surely die, because we have seen God.

The above passages were compiled in a book entitled *The New Topical Textbook*, edited by R. A. Torrey, published 1897. Many scholars who discuss Christ's Deity have compiled various verses from the Scriptures and some have juxtaposed them to show that the Lord Jesus Christ is God, our Creator. Many scholars have done tremendous works by putting verses side by side to show Christ's Deity. For example the compiled verses in *The New Topical Textbook*, a book edited by R. A. Torrey, published 1897.

Conclusion

The Lord Jesus Christ is God, Our Creator as Scriptures testify.

Activities for this Chapter

1. What do you think of the juxtaposed passages about Christ's Deity?

_____

_____

_____

_____

2. Which passages convince you the most about Christ's Deity?

_____

_____

_____

_____

- Which passages about Christ's Deity present challenges to you?

_____

_____

_____

_____

- Can you pray the LOD God to bring some light to you and clarify the passage or passages of the Scripture that present challenges to you?

- Have you accepted the Lord Jesus Christ as your LORD, God and your Savior?

_____

_____

_____

_____

- Would you like to invite the Lord Jesus Christ in your heart right now, in response to His invitation [Revelation 3:20]?

_____

_____

_____

_____

- What do you think of the passage of in Revelation 3:20?

_____

_____

_____

_____

- How about Revelation 1:8 and . . . . That say that the LORD Jesus Christ is God Almighty?

CHAPTER 9

The Work of the Holy Spirit

Now the earth was [a] formless and empty, darkness was over the surface of the deep, and the Spirit of God was hovering over the waters [Genesis 1:2].

The Holy Spirit is God, The Holy Spirit is the Spirit of the Lord Jesus Christ. The Holy Spirit reveals who the Lord Jesus Christ is, one would never know Who the Lord Jesus Christ Is, unless the Holy Spirit reveals the Lord to that person. The Lord Jesus Christ, The Father and the Holy Spirit are One. God is Sprit: God is spirit, and his worshipers must worship in the Spirit and in truth." [John 4:24]. The LORD Jesus Christ is God and He functions as the Father, the Son and the Holy Spirit. There is Only One God.

- The Holy Spirit reveals the Lord Jesus Christ:

Peter's confession: Simon Peter answered, "You are the Christ, the Son of the living God" [Matthew 16:16].

The Holy Spirit is the Breath of the Almighty,

The Holy Spirit is God since beginning:

[1] In the beginning God created the heavens and the earth. [2] Now the earth was formless and empty, darkness was over the surface of the deep, and the Spirit of God was hovering over the waters [Genesis 1:1-2].

Jesus Promises the Holy Spirit:

[15] "If you love me, keep my commands. [16] And I will ask the Father, and he will give you another advocate to help you and be with you forever—[17] the Spirit of truth. The world cannot accept him, because it neither sees him nor knows him. But you know him, for he lives with you and will be[c] in you. [18] I will not leave you as orphans; I will come to you. [19] Before long, the world will not see me anymore, but you will see me. Because I live, you also will live. [20] On that day you will realize that I am in my Father, and you are in me, and I am in you. [21] Whoever has my commands and keeps them is the one who loves me. The one who loves me will be loved by my Father, and I too will love them and show myself to them." The Holy Spirit reveals God [John14:15-24].

The Holy Spirit works for conversion: When he comes, he will prove the world to be in the wrong about sin and righteousness and judgment: [9] about sin, because people do not believe in me; [10] about righteousness, because I am going to the Father, where you can see me no longer; [11] and about judgment, because the prince of this world now stands condemned. [John 16:8]

The Lord Jesus takes the form of the Holy Spirit to enter in the heart of the Children's of God. The LORD said.

When I go, I will send the Holy Spirit, the Power, the Lord Jesus promises the Holy Spirit and He promised to be with the believers till the very end of the age: [John 14:15-21]. He promised to even be in the heart of the believers [John 14:20].

The Holy Spirit of God teaches about the LORD Jesus Christ: [John 15:26].

The best way to know a person is to listen to the person to hear what the person says, he or she is. In our discussions concerning Christ's Deity, the best way to know about WHO the LORD Jesus Christ IS, is to listen to Him and hear what the LORD says HE IS. It is very important to listen to what The LORD Jesus Christ says about Himself to well discuss His Deity. The LORD reveals His Deity in many passages in the Scriptures.

For examples, the LORD Jesus Christ says that He is God in several passages in the Bible:

- I and the Father are one" [John 10:30]

- Now this is eternal life: that they know you, the only true God, and Jesus Christ, whom you have sent. [John 17:3].

As for Matt Stick, he writes:

Jesus is God

by Matt Slick

"You are my witnesses," declares the LORD, "and my servant whom I have chosen, so that you may know and believe me and understand that I am he. Before me no god was formed, nor will there be one after me," (Isaiah 43:10).

| **JESUS** | **IS** | **GOD, "YAHWEH"** |

JESUS | **IS** | **GOD, "YAHWEH"**

John 1:3, "Through him all things were made; without him nothing was made that has been made."

Job 33:4, "The Spirit of God has made me; the breath of the Almighty gives me life."

Isaiah 40:28, "Do you not know? Have you not heard? The LORD is the everlasting God, the Creator of the ends of the earth. He will not grow tired or weary, and his understanding no one can fathom."

Creator

Col. 1:16-17, "For by him all things were created: things in heaven and on earth, visible and invisible, whether thrones or powers or rulers or authorities; all things were created by him and for him. He is before all things, and in him all things hold together."

Rev. 1:17, "When I saw him, I fell at his feet as though dead. Then he placed his right hand on me and said: 'Do not be afraid. I am the First and the Last.'"

Isaiah 41:4, "Who has done this and carried it through, calling forth the generations from the beginning? I, the LORD—with the first of them and with the last—I am he."

First and Last

Rev. 2:8, "To the angel of the church in Smyrna write: These are the words of him who is the First and the Last, who died and came to life again."

Isaiah 44:6, "This is what the LORD says—Israel's King and Redeemer, the LORD Almighty: I am the first and I am the last; apart from me there is no God."

Rev. 22:13, "I am the Alpha and the Omega, the First and the Last, the Beginning and the End."

Isaiah 48:12, "Listen to me, O Jacob, Israel, whom I have called: I am he; I am the first and I am the last."

John 8:24, "Therefore I said to you that you will die in your sins; for if you do not believe that I am He, you will die in your sins." (NKJV)

John 8:58, "I tell you the truth," Jesus answered, "before Abraham was born, I am!" See Exodus 3:14

John 13:19, "I am telling you now before it happens, so that when it does happen you will believe that I am He."

I AM

"ego eimi"

Exodus 3:14, "God said to Moses, "I AM WHO I AM. This is what you are to say to the Israelites: 'I AM has sent me to you.'"

Isaiah 43:10, "You are my witnesses," declares the LORD, "and my servant whom I have chosen, so that you may know and believe me and understand that I am he. Before me no god was formed, nor will there be one after me."

See also Deut. 32:39

Joel 3:12, "Let the nations be roused; let them advance into the Valley of Jehoshaphat, for there I will sit to judge all the nations on every side."

2 Tim. 4:1, "In the presence of God and of Christ Jesus, who will judge the living and the dead, and in view of his appearing and his kingdom, I give you this charge . . ."

2 Cor. 5:10, "For we must all appear before the judgment seat of Christ, that each one may receive what is due him for the things done while in the body, whether good or bad."

Judge

Rom. 14:10, "You, then, why do you judge your brother? Or why do you look down on your brother? For we will all stand before God's judgment seat."

Matt. 2:2, ". . . Where is the one who has been born king of the Jews? We saw his star in the east and have come to worship him."

Luke 23:3, "So Pilate asked Jesus, "Are you the king of the Jews?" "Yes, it is as you say," Jesus replied."

See also John 19:21

King

Jer. 10:10, "But the LORD is the true God; he is the living God, the eternal King. When he is angry, the earth trembles; the nations cannot endure his wrath."

Isaiah 44:6-8, "This is what the LORD says—Israel's King and Redeemer, the LORD Almighty: I am the first and I am the last; apart from me there is no God."

See also Psalm 47
Psalm 27:1, "The LORD is my light and my salvation—whom shall I fear?"

John 8:12, "When Jesus spoke again to the people, he said, "I am the light of the world. Whoever follows me will never walk in darkness, but will have the light of life."

Luke 2:32, "a light for revelation to the Gentiles and for glory to your people Israel."

See also John 1:7-9

Light

Isaiah 60:20, "our sun will never set again, and your moon will wane no more; the LORD will be your everlasting light, and your days of sorrow will end."

1 John 1:5, "God is light; in him there is no darkness at all."

1 Cor. 10:4, ". . . for they drank from the spiritual rock that accompanied them, and that rock was Christ."

See also 1 Pet. 2:4-8.

Rock

Deut. 32:4, "He is the Rock, his works are perfect, and all his ways are just. A faithful God who does no wrong, upright and just is he."

See also 2 Sam. 22:32 and Isaiah 17:10.

John 4:42, "They said to the woman, 'We no longer believe just because of what you said; now we have heard for ourselves, and we know that this man really is the Savior of the world.'"

1 John 4:14, "And we have seen and testify that the Father has sent his Son to be the Savior of the world."

Savior

Isaiah 43:3, "For I am the LORD, your God, the Holy One of Israel, your Savior"

Isaiah 45:21, ". . . And there is no God apart from me, a righteous God and a Savior; there is none but me."

John 10:11, "I am the good shepherd. The good shepherd lays down his life for the sheep."

Heb. 13:20, "May the God of peace, who through the blood of the eternal covenant brought back from the dead our Lord Jesus, that great Shepherd of the sheep,"

See also John 10:14,16; 1 Pet. 2:25

Shepherd

Psalm 23:1, "The LORD is my shepherd, I shall not be in want."

Isaiah 40:11, "He tends his flock like a shepherd: He gathers the lambs in his arms and carries them close to his heart; he gently leads those that have young."

Unless otherwise noted, all quotations are from the NASB.

What is so important here That the Lord Jesus Christ claimed to be God (John 5:18; 8:24; 8:58—see Exodus 3:14) and the only way to salvation (John 14:6). If He really did rise from the dead and perform those miracles, then what He said about Himself—and who He claimed to be—become vitally important.

The Lord Jesus Christ is the Word of God Who became flesh to save us: [John 1-15].

In this passage we learn that the Word became flesh and the Word was with God.

The Earthly Ministry of the Lord Jesus Christ.

During his earthly ministry when the Lord came to minister on earth, His birth was announced by prophesies.

The LORD took on Flesh and He was conceived by the power of the Holy Spirit and He was called powerful names that point to His Deity and His Mighty and His Sovereignty:

- The Lord's birth was predicted as we read in the Scriptures. For examples:

- For to us a child is born, to us a son is given, and the government will be on his shoulders. And he will be called Wonderful Counselor, Mighty God, Everlasting Father, and Prince of Peace [Isaiah 9:6].

- Of the increase of his government and peace there will be no end. He will reign on David's throne and over his kingdom, establishing and upholding it with justice and righteousness from that time on and forever. The zeal of the LORD Almighty will accomplish this [Isaiah 9:7].

- 21She will give birth to a son, and you are to give him the name Jesus,[f] because he will save his people from their sins."

   22 All this took place to fulfill what the Lord had said through the prophet: 23 "The virgin will conceive and give birth to a son, and they will call him Immanuel"[g] (which means "God with us") [Matthew 1:21-23].

Scriptures have provided details about the Messiah's birthplace, (Bethlehem), would be born of a virgin, He would and that the Messiah would be God Himself and so forth.

- *The savior would be born in Bethlehem:* "O Bethlehem Ephrathah, though you are little among the thousands of Judah, yet out of you shall come forth to Me The One to be Ruler in Israel, whose goings forth are from of old, from everlasting [Micah 5:2].

- *He would be born of a virgin:* "Behold! The virgin shall conceive and bear a Son, and shall call His name Immanuel" [Isaiah 7:14].

- *The savior would be God Himself:* "unto us a Child is born, unto us a Son is given. And the government will be upon His shoulder. And His name will be called Wonderful, Counselor, Mighty God, Everlasting Father, Prince of Peace! (Isaiah 9:6)

- *He would be a sacrifice for our sins:* "Surely He has borne our grief and carried our sorrows; Yet we esteemed Him stricken, Smitten by God, and afflicted. But He was wounded for our transgressions, He was bruised for our iniquities. (Isaiah 53:4) "By His knowledge My righteous Servant shall justify many, For He shall bear their iniquities. Therefore I will divide Him a portion with the great, And He shall divide the spoil with the strong. Because He poured out His soul unto death, And He was numbered with the transgressors, And He bore the sin of many, And made intercession for the transgressors" [Isaiah 53:10-12].

- *The savior would be resurrected:* "For You will not leave my soul in Sheol, nor will You allow Your Holy One to see corruption. (Psalm 16:10)

- *His sacrifice would bring us peace with God:* "The chastisement for our peace was upon Him, and by His stripes we are healed" [Isaiah 53:5].

- The Lord was conceived by the Holy Spirit:

He was called Jesus, which means he would save His people from sins:

> She will give birth to a son, and you are to give him the name Jesus,[f] because he will save his people from their sins" [Matthew 1:21].

The LORD was also called Immanuel, which means God with us:

> [22] All this took place to fulfill what the Lord had said through the prophet: [23] "The virgin will conceive and give birth to a son, and they will call him Immanuel"[g] (which means "God with us") [Matthew 1:23].

- The LORD told to Philip that He is the Father: [Matthew 14:9].

- The Lord says: He and the father are One [John 10:30].

> [9] Jesus answered: "Don't you know me, Philip, even after I have been among you such a long time? Anyone who has seen me has seen the Father. How can you say, 'Show us the Father'? [10] Don't you believe that I am in the Father, and that the Father is in me? The words I say to you I do not speak on my own authority. Rather, it is the Father, living in me, who is doing his work. [11] Believe me when I say that I am in the Father and the Father is in me; or at least believe on the evidence of the works themselves [John 14:9].

Conclusion

There is Only One God as Scriptures teach us and as the Lord Jesus Christ Himself confirms.

> "Hear, O Israel! Yahweh is our God, Yahweh is one!" [Deuteronomy 6:4].

The Lord stated explained that before Abraham was, He IS:

> "I tell you the truth," Jesus answered, "before Abraham was born, I am!" [John8:58].

Activities for this Chapter.

1. What is the work of the Holy Spirit?

_____

_____

_____

_____

2. Who Is the Holy Spirit?

_____

_____

_____

_____

3 Who gives the Holy Spirit and what is the work of the Holy Spirit?

_____

_____

_____

_____

CHAPTER 10

Juxtaposed Scriptures that Discuss Christ's Deity: Passages from the Old Testament and Passages from the New Testament.

Sanctify them by[d] the truth; your word is truth [John 17:17]. The word of God is truth, prior to concluding the contents of this book, I would like to invite the audience to consider the following juxtapositions of passages from From the Old Testament and from the New Testament that discuss the nature and the identity of God. While we are reading, let us remember that God is Truth and His word is truth [John 17:17]; [John 14:6].

Having established this fundamental truth God's truth and the truth of His Word, let us now examine the juxtaposed verses from the Scriptures in the Holy Bible.

The first table of juxtaposition is presented by Reverend Matt Slick; it is a more elaborated table as the writer has juxtaposed passages from the Scriptures to draw parallelism and to show that God Almighty of the Old Testament is the same God Almighty of the New Testament and that there is Only One God. The second table is a summary of some powerful arguments surrounding Christ's Deity that most scholars have pointed out in their discussions. I have tried to highlight these arguments in table 2 by recalling and examining arguments other scholars have presented. Although the arguments in table 2 are the most considered ones, there may be others that are left out. Once again, the arguments I summarize have been used by other scholars, they present passages from the Bible to educate. I have modified lines, but they are all the word of God. This is a scholarly discussion and I draw ideas from other scholars for education purpose to educate the people of God. Those arguments about Christ's Deity or the Deity the Lord Jesus Christ include: the prophesies, the worship issue, the healing power and the power to create to mention but these. The third set of verses present a juxtaposition of verses that show that the Lord Jesus Christ is God. These are verses from the Scriptures and anyone can read them in the Holy Bible.

Table 1, by Reverend Matt Slick.

• **Jesus is God**

JESUS	IS	GOD, "YAHWEH"
John 1:3, "Through him all things were made; without him nothing was made that has been made."		Job 33:4, "The Spirit of God has made me; the breath of the Almighty gives me life."
Col. 1:16-17, "For by him all things were created: things in heaven and on earth, visible and invisible, whether thrones or powers or rulers or authorities; all things were created by him and for him. He is before all things, and in him all things hold together."	**Creator**	Isaiah 40:28, "Do you not know? Have you not heard? The LORD is the everlasting God, the Creator of the ends of the earth. He will not grow tired or weary, and his understanding no one can fathom."
5Rev. 1:17, "When I saw him, I fell at his feet as though dead. Then he placed his right hand on me and said: 'Do not be afraid. I am the First and the Last.'"		Isaiah 41:4, "Who has done this and carried it through, calling forth the generations from the beginning? I, the LORD—with the first of them and with the last—I am he."
Rev. 2:8, "To the angel of the church in Smyrna write: These are the words of him who is the First and the Last, who died and came to life again."	**First and Last**	Isaiah 44:6, "This is what the LORD says—Israel's King and Redeemer, the LORD Almighty: I am the first and I am the last; apart from me there is no God."
Rev. 22:13, "I am the Alpha and the Omega, the First and the Last, the Beginning and the End."		Isaiah 48:12, "Listen to me, O Jacob, Israel, whom I have called: I am he; I am the first and I am the last."

John 8:24, "Therefore I said to you that you will die in your sins; for if you do not believe that I am He, you will die in your sins." (NKJV)

John 8:58, "I tell you the truth," Jesus answered, "before Abraham was born, I am!" See Exodus 3:14

John 13:19, "I am telling you now before it happens, so that when it does happen you will believe that I am He."

I AM

"ego eimi"

Exodus 3:14, "God said to Moses, "I AM WHO I AM. This is what you are to say to the Israelites: 'I AM has sent me to you.'"

Isaiah 43:10, "You are my witnesses," declares the LORD, "and my servant whom I have chosen, so that you may know and believe me and understand that I am he. Before me no god was formed, nor will there be one after me."

See also Deut. 32:39

Joel 3:12, "Let the nations be roused; let them advance into the Valley of Jehoshaphat, for there I will sit to judge all the nations on every side."

2 Tim. 4:1, "In the presence of God and of Christ Jesus, who will judge the living and the dead, and in view of his appearing and his kingdom, I give you this charge . . ."

2 Cor. 5:10, "For we must all appear before the judgment seat of Christ, that each one may receive what is due him for the things done while in the body, whether good or bad."

Matt. 2:2, ". . . Where is the one who has been born king of the Jews? We saw his star in the east and have come to worship him."

Judge

Rom. 14:10, "You, then, why do you judge your brother? Or why do you look down on your brother? For we will all stand before God's judgment seat."

Jer. 10:10, "But the LORD is the true God; he is the living God, the eternal King. When he is angry, the earth trembles; the nations cannot endure his wrath."

Luke 23:3, "So Pilate asked Jesus, "Are you the king of the Jews?" "Yes, it is as you say," Jesus replied."

See also John 19:21

King

Isaiah 44:6-8, "This is what the LORD says—Israel's King and Redeemer, the LORD Almighty: I am the first and I am the last; apart from me there is no God."

See also Psalm 47

John 8:12, "When Jesus spoke again to the people, he said, "I am the light of the world. Whoever follows me will never walk in darkness, but will have the light of life."

Luke 2:32, "a light for revelation to the Gentiles and for glory to your people Israel."

See also John 1:7-9

Light

Psalm 27:1, "The LORD is my light and my salvation—whom shall I fear?"

Isaiah 60:20, "our sun will never set again, and your moon will wane no more; the LORD will be your everlasting light, and your days of sorrow will end."

1 John 1:5, "God is light; in him there is no darkness at all."

1 Cor. 10:4, ". . . for they drank from the spiritual rock that accompanied them, and that rock was Christ."

See also 1 Pet. 2:4-8.

Rock

Deut. 32:4, "He is the Rock, his works are perfect, and all his ways are just. A faithful God who does no wrong, upright and just is he."

See also 2 Sam. 22:32 and Isaiah 17:10.

John 4:42, "They said to the woman, 'We no longer believe just because of what you said; now we have heard for ourselves, and we know that this man really is the Savior of the world.'"

1 John 4:14, "And we have seen and testify that the Father has sent his Son to be the Savior of the world."

Savior

Isaiah 43:3, "For I am the LORD, your God, the Holy One of Israel, your Savior"

Isaiah 45:21, ". . . And there is no God apart from me, a righteous God and a Savior; there is none but me."

John 10:11, "I am the good shepherd. The good shepherd lays down his life for the sheep."

Heb. 13:20, "May the God of peace, who through the blood of the eternal covenant brought back from the dead our Lord Jesus, that great Shepherd of the sheep,"

See also John 10:14,16; 1 Pet. 2:25

Shepherd

Psalm 23:1, "The LORD is my shepherd, I shall not be in want."

Isaiah 40:11, "He tends his flock like a shepherd: He gathers the lambs in his arms and carries them close to his heart; he gently leads those that have young."

Table 2. The Summary of arguments and passages from Scriptures that most scholars consider in the discussions about Christ's Deity.

Among many other arguments most scholars put forwards to discuss Christ's Deity are the following:

1.   Unchanging Nature

God	Jesus

God
 	
  • *God never changes.*
 	
Malachi 3:6 For I am the LORD, I change not; therefore ye sons of Jacob are not consumed.
	Jesus
	
	  • *Jesus never changes.*
	
	Hebrews 13:8 Jesus Christ the same yesterday, and to day, and for ever.

2.   Power to give Salvation

God	Jesus
God *God is the only Saviour.* "I, even I, am the LORD; and beside me there is no saviour." Isaiah 43:11 To the only wise God our Saviour . . . Jude 1:12 God our Saviour. Titus 2:10 . . . we trust in the living God, who is the Saviour. I Timothy 4:10 God my Saviour. Luke 1:47	Jesus Jesus is the only Saviour. . . . the Father sent the Son to be the Saviour of the world. 1 John 4:14 . . . our Lord and Saviour Jesus Christ. II Peter 3:18 . . . God and our Saviour Jesus Christ. II Peter 1:1 . . . the Christ, the Saviour of the world. John 4:42

	. . . the Lord Jesus Christ our Saviour. Titus 1:4 a Saviour, which is Christ the Lord. Luke 2:11
	Neither is there salvation in any other (than Jesus): for there is none other name under heaven given among men, whereby we must be saved.
	—Acts 4:12
	. . . salvation . . . is in Christ Jesus with eternal glory.
	—2 Timothy 2:10
	. . . captain of their salvation [Jesus] perfect through sufferings.
	—Heb 2:10
	[Jesus] . . . author of eternal salvation . . .
	—Heb 5:9

3.   Power to Forgive Sins

• Forgiveness of Sins	• Forgiveness of Sins
God forgives sins.	Jesus forgives sins.
[T]he Lord . . . forgiveth all thine iniquities . . . Psalm 103:2-3	Jesus . . . said . . . "Son, thy sins be forgiven thee." Mark 2:5
"[W]ho can forgive sins but God only?" Mark	

4.   Power to Redeem people from sins

• Power to Redeem	• Power to Redeem
God is our redeemer.	Jesus redeemed us.
[T]hou, O LORD, art our father, our redeemer. Isaiah 63:16	[T]the great God and our Saviour Jesus Christ . . . gave himself for us, that he might redeem us from all iniquity. Titus 2:13-14

5.   The Oneness of God

God is one.	Jesus and God are one.
Hear, O Israel: The LORD our God is one LORD. Deuteronomy 6:4	I and my Father are one. John 10:30 In the beginning was the Word, and the Word was with God, and the Word was God . . . All things were made by him . . . He was in the world, and the world was made by him, and the world knew him not . . . And the Word was made flesh, and dwelt among us John 1:1, 3, 10, 14 Jesus saith . . . he that hath seen me hath seen the Father; and how sayest thou then, Shew us the Father? John 14:9 For there are three that bear record in heaven, the Father, the Word, and the Holy Ghost: and these three are one. 1 John 5:7

6.   The Son ship

God has a Son.	Jesus is God's Son.
[T]he LORD hath said unto me, Thou art my Son; this day have I begotten thee. Psalms 2:7	. . . [Jesus] said also that God was his Father . . . John 5:18

7.   Holiness

• Holiness	• Holiness
God is the Holy One	Jesus is the Holy One.
Psalms 71:22 I will also praise thee with the psaltery, even thy truth, O my God: unto thee will I sing with the harp, O thou Holy One of Israel.	Acts 2:27 Because thou wilt not leave my soul in hell, neither wilt thou suffer thine Holy One to see corruption.
Psalms 78:41 Yea, they turned back and tempted God, and limited the Holy One of Israel.	
Psalms 89:18 For the LORD is our defence; and the Holy One of Israel is our king.	

Isaiah 10:20 And it shall come to pass in that day, that the remnant of Israel, and such as are escaped of the house of Jacob, shall no more again stay upon him that smote them; but shall stay upon the LORD, the Holy One of Israel, in truth.	3:13-14 The God of Abraham, and of Isaac, and of Jacob, the God of our fathers, hath glorified his Son Jesus; whom ye delivered up, and denied him in the presence of Pilate, when he was determined to let him go. But ye denied the Holy One and the Just, and desired a murderer to be granted unto you;
Psalms 16:10 For thou wilt not leave my soul in hell; neither wilt thou suffer thine Holy One to see corruption. (Messianic Psalm)	13:34-35 And as concerning that he raised him up from the dead, now no more to return to corruption, he said on this wise, I will give you the sure mercies of David. Wherefore he saith also in another psalm, Thou shalt not suffer thine Holy One to see corruption.

8.   Power to Create

God	Jesus
God created the universe and earth by Himself.	Jesus Christ created the universe and the earth.
I am the LORD that maketh all things; that stretcheth forth the heavens alone; that spreadeth abroad the earth by myself. Isaiah 44:24	[U]nto the Son he saith . . . Thou, LORD, in the beginning hast laid the foundation of the earth; and the heavens are the works of thine hands. Hebrews 1:10

In the beginning God created the heaven and the earth. Genesis 1:1	[B]y him [Jesus] were all things created, that are in heaven, and that are in earth . . . all things were created by him, and for him. Colossians 1:16 All things were made by him; and without him was not anything made that was made. John 1:3

9.   Word

God is the Word. In the beginning was the Word, and the Word was with God, and the Word was God John 1:1	Jesus is the Word. . . . the Word was made flesh, and dwelt among us . . . John 1:14

10.   The First and the Last

God is the first and the last. I the LORD, the first, and with the last; I am he. Isaiah 41:4	Jesus is the first and the last. Jesus said, "Fear not; I am the first and the last:" Revelation 1:17

11.   Worthy to Be Worshipped

Only God is worshipped. . . . Then saith Jesus unto him . . . Thou shalt worship the Lord thy God, and him only shalt thou serve. Matthew 4:10	Jesus is worshipped. While [Jesus] spake these things unto them, behold, there came a certain ruler, and worshipped him . . . Matthew 9:18 And again, when [God] bringeth in the firstbegotten [Jesus] into the world, he saith, And let all the angels of God worship him. Hebrews 1:6 And Thomas answered and said unto [Jesus], My Lord and my God. John 20:28

12.   Messiah

God is Messiah. . . . unto us a child is born, unto us a son is given: and the government shall be upon his shoulder . . . and his name shall be called . . . The mighty God, The everlasting Father . . . Isaiah 9:6	Jesus is Messiah. The woman saith unto him, I know that Messias cometh, which is called Christ: when he is come, he will tell us all things. Jesus saith unto her, I that speak unto thee am he. John 4:25-26

13.   From Everlasting

God	Jesus
God is from everlasting. The LORD reigneth, he is clothed with majesty; the LORD is clothed with strength, wherewith he hath girded himself: the world also is stablished, that it cannot be moved. Thy throne is established of old: thou art from everlasting. Psalms 93:1-2	Messiah Yeshua [Jesus] is from everlasting. But thou, Bethlehem Ephratah . . . out of thee shall he come forth unto me that is to be ruler in Israel; whose goings forth have been from of old, from everlasting. Micah 5:2

14.   Glorification

God	Jesus
Only God is glorified. I am the LORD: that is my name: and my glory will I not give to another . . . Isaiah 42:8	God glorified Jesus. And now, O Father, glorify thou me with thine own self with the glory which I had with thee before the world was. John 17:5 [A]ll men should honour the Son, even as they honour the Father. He that honoureth not the Son honoureth not the Father which hath sent him. John 5:23

	But unto the Son he [God] saith, Thy throne, O God, is for ever and ever: a sceptre of righteousness is the sceptre of thy kingdom. Hebrews 1:8

15. "The Great I AM"

God	Jesus
God is 'I am'.	Jesus is 'I am'.
And God said unto Moses, I AM THAT I AM: and he said, Thus shalt thou say unto the children of Israel, I AM hath sent me unto you. Exodus 3:14	Jesus said unto them, Verily, verily, I say unto you, Before Abraham was, I am. John 8:58

16. Healing Power

God	Jesus
God heals all diseases.	Jesus heals all diseases.
Bless the LORD . . . who healeth all thy diseases. Psalms 103:2	[Jesus] healed all that were sick. Matthew 8:16

17.   Judge of All Mankind.

God	Jesus
God is the Judge of the whole earth.	Jesus is the Judge of the whole earth.
O Lord God, to whom vengeance belongeth; O God, to whom vengeance belongeth, shew thyself. Lift up thyself, thou judge of the earth: render a reward to the proud. Psalms 94:1-2	[T]he Father judgeth no man, but hath committed all judgment unto the Son: John 5:22
[Abraham to God] . . . Shall not the Judge of all the earth do right? Genesis 18:25	

18.   Having LIFE in Oneself

God	Jesus
God has life in Himself.	Jesus has life in Himself. so hath [God] given to the Son to have life in himself;
[T]he Father hath life in himself; John 5:26	
	In [Jesus] was life; and the life was the light of men. John 1:4

19.   Power to Raise the dead

God	Jesus
God raises the dead.	Jesus raises the dead.
[T]he Father raiseth up the dead, and quickeneth them; John 5:21	[T]he Son quickeneth whom he will. John 5:21

We can draw some powerful conclusion based on the evidence provided by the passages. The Lord Jesus Christ is God as the Scriptures instruct us. As we can also see the Scriptures cannot be wrong.

2. Table of the summary statements and verses from the Scriptures that most scholars consider in the discussions about Christ's Deity:

Other passages from the Holy Bible that show that the Lord Jesus Christ is God include the following:

1. Revelation 1:7-8 Jesus was the Almighty.
2. Genesis 17:1 And the Almighty was God.

1. John 8:58 Jesus was the "I Am"
2. Exodus 3:14 and the "I Am" was God

1. Acts 3:14 Jesus was the "HOLY ONE"
2. Isaiah 43:15 and the "HOLY ONE" was God

1. John 8:24 Jesus is the "I Am He"
2. Isaiah 43:10 and the "I Am He" was God

1. Revelation 22:13 Jesus is the "First and the Last"
2. Isaiah 44:6 and the "First and the Last" was God

1. I Corinthians 10:4 Jesus was "The Rock"
2. Psalm 18:31 and "The Rock" was God

1. II Corinthians 11:2 Jesus was the "One HUSBAND"
2. Jeremiah 31:32 and the "One HUSBAND" was God

1. Matthew 23:8 Jesus was the "ONE MASTER"
2. Malachi 1:6 and the "ONE MASTER" was God

1. John 10:16 Jesus was the "One SHEPHERD"
2. Isaiah 40:11 and the "ONE SHEPHERD" was God

1. Acts 4:12 Jesus was the "ONE SAVIOR"
2. Isaiah 45:21 and the "ONE SAVIOR" was God

1. Luke 1:68 Jesus was the "ONE REDEEMER"
2. Isaiah 41:14 and the "ONE REDEEMER" was God

1. Revelation 19:16 Jesus was "LORD OF LORDS"
2. Timothy 6:14 Jesus was "LORD OF LORDS"

1. Deuteronomy 10:17 and the "LORD OF LORDS" was God
2. Philippians 2:10 Every knee must bow to Jesus

1. Isaiah 45:23 Every knee must bow to God
2. John 1: 3-10 Jesus was the "ONE Creator"

1. Isaiah 44:24 Jesus was the "ONE Creator"
2. Genesis. 1:1 and the "ONE Creator" was God

1. John 1:49 Jesus was "KING OF ISRAEL"
2. Isaiah 44:6 and the "KING OF ISRAEL" was God

1. Deuteronomy 4:35 The Lord He is God, there is NONE else beside him
2. Deuteronomy 4:39 there is None Else

1. Deuteronomy 6:4 the Lord our God is ONE Lord
2. Deuteronomy 32:39 I even I, am He and

1. THERE IS NO GOD WITH ME
2. 1 Kings 8:60 The LORD is God—There is None Else

1. Kings 19:15 You ALONE are the only true God
2. Psalm 86:10 You are God, YOU ALONE

1. Isaiah 40:8 I am Jehovah, and to no one else shall I give my own glory
2. Isaiah 43:10,11 Before me there was no God formed

1. NEITHER SHALL THERE BE AFTER ME. I,
2. EVEN I AM THE LORD: AND BESIDE ME THERE IS NO SAVIOR.

1. Isaiah 44:6 I AM THE FIRST, AND THE LAST: AND BESIDE ME THERE IS NO GOD
2. Isaiah 45:5 I am the Lord, and there is NONE ELSE, THERE IS NO GOD BESIDE ME

1. Isaiah 45:6 There is NONE beside Me.
2. I am the Lord and there is NONE else.

1. Isaiah 45:15 you are a God, the /God of Israel, a Savior.
2. Isaiah 45:22 turn to me and be saved.

1. For I am God, and there is no one else
2. Isaiah 48:11 I will not give my glory unto another. Isaiah 45:5

1. Isaiah 48:12 I am he, I am the first,
2. I also am the Last. Revelation 1:8

1. Hosea 13:4 I am Jehovah your God, there was no God except me, and there was no savior but I.
2. Joel 2:27 I am your God, and None Else

1. Zechariah 14:9 In that day shall there be ONE LORD AND HIS NAME ONE
2. Philippians 2:11 that Jesus Christ is Lord, to the Glory of God the Father

1. Matthew 23:9 For one is your Father, the heavenly one
2. Mark 12:29 Jehovah our God is one Jehovah

3. Scriptures compiled by R.A Torrey for teaching purpose in *The New Topical Textbook*, edited by R. A. Torrey, published 1897.

For his part, R.A. Torrey has presented a list of powerful passages from the Scripture to show that the Lord Jesus Christ is God as we read in *The New Topical Textbook,* edited by R. A. Torrey, published 1897.

CHRIST IS GOD

- As Jehovah.

  Isaiah 40:3 The voice of him that crieth in the wilderness, Prepare ye the way of the LORD, make straight in the desert a highway for our God.

  Matthew 3:3 For this is he that was spoken of by the prophet Esaias, saying, The voice of one crying in the wilderness, Prepare ye the way of the Lord, make his paths straight.

- As Jehovah of glory.

  Psalms 24:7 Lift up your heads, O ye gates; and be ye lift up, ye everlasting doors; and the King of glory shall come in.

  Psalms 24:10 Who is this King of glory? The LORD of hosts, he *is* the King of glory. Selah.

  1 Corinthians 2:8 Which none of the princes of this world knew: for had they known *it,* they would not have crucified the Lord of glory.

James 2:1 My brethren, have not the faith of our Lord Jesus Christ, *the Lord* of glory, with respect of persons.

- As Jehovah, our RIGHTEOUSNESS.

Jeremiah 23:5-6 Behold, the days come, saith the LORD, that I will raise unto David a righteous Branch, and a King shall reign and prosper, and shall execute judgment and justice in the earth. In his days Judah shall be saved, and Israel shall dwell safely: and this *is* his name whereby he shall be called, THE LORD OUR RIGHTEOUSNESS.

1 Corinthians 1:30 But of him are ye in Christ Jesus, who of God is made unto us wisdom, and righteousness, and sanctification, and redemption:

- As Jehovah, above all.

Psalms 97:9 For thou, LORD, *art* high above all the earth: thou art exalted far above all gods.

John 3:31 He that cometh from above is above all: he that is of the earth is earthly, and speaketh of the earth: he that cometh from heaven is above all.

- As Jehovah, the First and the Last.

Isaiah 44:6 Thus saith the LORD the King of Israel, and his redeemer the LORD of hosts; I *am* the first, and I *am* the last; and beside me *there is* no God.

Revelation 1:17 And when I saw him, I fell at his feet as dead. And he laid his right hand upon me, saying unto me, Fear not; I am the first and the last:

Isaiah 48:12-16 Hearken unto me, O Jacob and Israel, my called; I *am* he; I *am* the first, I also *am* the last. Mine hand also hath laid the foundation of the earth, and my right hand hath spanned the

heavens: *when* I call unto them, they stand up together. All ye, assemble yourselves, and hear; which among them hath declared these *things?* The LORD hath loved him: he will do his pleasure on Babylon, and his arm *shall be on* the Chaldeans. I, *even* I, have spoken; yea, I have called him: I have brought him, and he shall make his way prosperous. Come ye near unto me, hear ye this; I have not spoken in secret from the beginning; from the time that it was, there *am* I: and now the Lord GOD, and his Spirit, hath sent me . . . .

Revelation 22:13 I am Alpha and Omega, the beginning and the end, the first and the last.

- As Jehovah's Fellow and Equal.

Zechariah 13:7 Awake, O sword, against my shepherd, and against the man *that is* my fellow, saith the LORD of hosts: smite the shepherd, and the sheep shall be scattered: and I will turn mine hand upon the little ones.

Philippians 2:6 Who, being in the form of God, thought it not robbery to be equal with God:

- As Jehovah of Hosts.

Isaiah 6:1-3 In the year that king Uzziah died I saw also the Lord sitting upon a throne, high and lifted up, and his train filled the temple. Above it stood the seraphims: each one had six wings; with twain he covered his face, and with twain he covered his feet, and with twain he did fly. And one cried unto another, and said, Holy, holy, holy, *is* the LORD of hosts: the whole earth *is* full of his glory.

John 12:41 These things said Esaias, when he saw his glory, and spake of him.

Isaiah 8:13-14 Sanctify the LORD of hosts himself; and *let* him *be* your fear, and *let* him *be* your dread. And he shall be for a

sanctuary; but for a stone of stumbling and for a rock of offence to both the houses of Israel, for a gin and for a snare to the inhabitants of Jerusalem.

1 Peter 2:8 And a stone of stumbling, and a rock of offence, *even to them* which stumble at the word, being disobedient: whereunto also they were appointed.

- As Jehovah, the Shepherd.

Isaiah 40:11 He shall feed his flock like a shepherd: he shall gather the lambs with his arm, and carry *them* in his bosom, *and* shall gently lead those that are with young.

Hebrews 13:20 Now the God of peace, that brought again from the dead our Lord Jesus, that great shepherd of the sheep, through the blood of the everlasting covenant,

- As Jehovah, for whose glory all things were created.

Proverbs 16:4 The LORD hath made all *things* for himself: yea, even the wicked for the day of evil.

Colossians 1:16 For by him were all things created, that are in heaven, and that are in earth, visible and invisible, whether *they be* thrones, or dominions, or principalities, or powers: all things were created by him, and for him:

- As Jehovah, the Messenger of the covenant.

Malachi 3:1 Behold, I will send my messenger, and he shall prepare the way before me: and the Lord, whom ye seek, shall suddenly come to his temple, even the messenger of the covenant, whom ye delight in: behold, he shall come, saith the LORD of hosts.

Mark 1:2 As it is written in the prophets, Behold, I send my messenger before thy face, which shall prepare thy way before thee.

Luke 2:27 And he came by the Spirit into the temple: and when the parents brought in the child Jesus, to do for him after the custom of the law,

- Invoked as Jehovah.

Joel 2:32 And it shall come to pass, *that* whosoever shall call on the name of the LORD shall be delivered: for in mount Zion and in Jerusalem shall be deliverance, as the LORD hath said, and in the remnant whom the LORD shall call.

Acts 2:21 And it shall come to pass, *that* whosoever shall call on the name of the Lord shall be saved.

1 Corinthians 1:2 Unto the church of God which is at Corinth, to them that are sanctified in Christ Jesus, called *to be* saints, with all that in every place call upon the name of Jesus Christ our Lord, both theirs and ours:

- As the Eternal God and Creator.

Psalms 102:24-27 I said, O my God, take me not away in the midst of my days: thy years *are* throughout all generations. Of old hast thou laid the foundation of the earth: and the heavens *are* the work of thy hands. They shall perish, but thou shalt endure: yea, all of them shall wax old like a garment; as a vesture shalt thou change them, and they shall be changed: But thou *art* the same, and thy years shall have no end.

Hebrews 1:8 But unto the Son *he saith*, Thy throne, O God, *is* for ever and ever: a sceptre of righteousness *is* the sceptre of thy kingdom.

Hebrews 1:10-12 And, Thou, Lord, in the beginning hast laid the foundation of the earth; and the heavens are the works of thine hands: They shall perish; but thou remainest; and they all shall wax old as doth a garment; And as a vesture shalt thou fold them up, and they shall be changed: but thou art the same, and thy years shall not fail.

- As the mighty God.

Isaiah 9:6 For unto us a child is born, unto us a son is given: and the government shall be upon his shoulder: and his name shall be called Wonderful, Counsellor, The mighty God, The everlasting Father, The Prince of Peace.

- As the Great God and Saviour.

Hosea 1:7 But I will have mercy upon the house of Judah, and will save them by the LORD their God, and will not save them by bow, nor by sword, nor by battle, by horses, nor by horsemen.

Titus 2:13 Looking for that blessed hope, and the glorious appearing of the great God and our Saviour Jesus Christ;

- As God over all.

Psalms 45:6-7 Thy throne, O God, *is* for ever and ever: the sceptre of thy kingdom *is* a right sceptre. Thou lovest righteousness, and hatest wickedness: therefore God, thy God, hath anointed thee with the oil of gladness above thy fellows.

- As the true God.

Jeremiah 10:10 But the LORD *is* the true God, he *is* the living God, and an everlasting king: at his wrath the earth shall tremble, and the nations shall not be able to abide his indignation.

1 John 5:20 And we know that the Son of God is come, and hath given us an understanding, that we may know him that is true, and we are in him that is true, *even* in his Son Jesus Christ. This is the true God, and eternal life.

- As God the Word.

John 1:1 In the beginning was the Word, and the Word was with God, and the Word was God.

- As God, the Judge.

Ecclesiastes 12:14 For God shall bring every work into judgment, with every secret thing, whether *it be* good, or whether *it be* evil.

1 Corinthians 4:5 Therefore judge nothing before the time, until the Lord come, who both will bring to light the hidden things of darkness, and will make manifest the counsels of the hearts: and then shall every man have praise of God.

2 Corinthians 5:10 For we must all appear before the judgment seat of Christ; that every one may receive the things *done* in *his* body, according to that he hath done, whether *it be* good or bad.

2 Timothy 4:1 I charge *thee* therefore before God, and the Lord Jesus Christ, who shall judge the quick and the dead at his appearing and his kingdom;

- As Emmanuel.

Isaiah 7:14 Therefore the Lord himself shall give you a sign; Behold, a virgin shall conceive, and bear a son, and shall call his name Immanuel.

Matthew 1:23 Behold, a virgin shall be with child, and shall bring forth a son, and they shall call his name Emmanuel, which being interpreted is, God with us.

- As King of kings and Lord of lords.

Daniel 10:17 For how can the servant of this my lord talk with this my lord? for as for me, straightway there remained no strength in me, neither is there breath left in me.

Revelation 1:5 And from Jesus Christ, *who is* the faithful witness, *and* the first begotten of the dead, and the prince of the kings of the earth. Unto him that loved us, and washed us from our sins in his own blood,

Revelation 17:14 These shall make war with the Lamb, and the Lamb shall overcome them: for he is Lord of lords, and King of kings: and they that are with him *are* called, and chosen, and faithful.

• As the Holy One.

1 Samuel 2:2 *There is* none holy as the LORD: for *there is* none beside thee: neither *is there* any rock like our God.

Acts 3:14 But ye denied the Holy One and the Just, and desired a murderer to be granted unto you;

• As the Lord from heaven.

1 Corinthians 15:47 The first man *is* of the earth, earthy: the second man *is* the Lord from heaven.

• As Lord of the sabbath.

Genesis 2:3 And God blessed the seventh day, and sanctified it: because that in it he had rested from all his work which God created and made.

Matthew 12:8 For the Son of man is Lord even of the sabbath day.

• As Lord of all.

Acts 10:36 The word which *God* sent unto the children of Israel, preaching peace by Jesus Christ: (he is Lord of all:)

Romans 10:11-13 For the scripture saith, Whosoever believeth on him shall not be ashamed. For there is no difference between the Jew and the Greek: for the same Lord over all is rich unto all that call upon him. For whosoever shall call upon the name of the Lord shall be saved.

- As Son of God.

Matthew 26:63-67 But Jesus held his peace. And the high priest answered and said unto him, I adjure thee by the living God, that thou tell us whether thou be the Christ, the Son of God. Jesus saith unto him, Thou hast said: nevertheless I say unto you, Hereafter shall ye see the Son of man sitting on the right hand of power, and coming in the clouds of heaven. Then the high priest rent his clothes, saying, He hath spoken blasphemy; what further need have we of witnesses? behold, now ye have heard his blasphemy. What think ye? They answered and said, He is guilty of death. Then did they spit in his face, and buffeted him; and others smote *him* with the palms of their hands, . . .

- As the Only-begotten Son of the Father.

John 1:14 And the Word was made flesh, and dwelt among us, (and we beheld his glory, the glory as of the only begotten of the Father,) full of grace and truth.

John 3:16 For God so loved the world, that he gave his only begotten Son, that whosoever believeth in him should not perish, but have everlasting life.

John 3:18 He that believeth on him is not condemned: but he that believeth not is condemned already, because he hath not believed in the name of the only begotten Son of God.

1 John 4:9 In this was manifested the love of God toward us, because that God sent his only begotten Son into the world, that we might live through him.

- His blood is called the blood of God.

  Acts 20:28 Take heed therefore unto yourselves, and to all the flock, over the which the Holy Ghost hath made you overseers, to feed the church of God, which he hath purchased with his own blood.

- As one with the Father.

  John 10:30 I and *my* Father are one.

  John 12:45 And he that seeth me seeth him that sent me.

  John 14:7-10 If ye had known me, ye should have known my Father also: and from henceforth ye know him, and have seen him. Philip saith unto him, Lord, shew us the Father, and it sufficeth us. Jesus saith unto him, Have I been so long time with you, and yet hast thou not known me, Philip? he that hath seen me hath seen the Father; and how sayest thou *then*, Shew us the Father? Believest thou not that I am in the Father, and the Father in me? the words that I speak unto you I speak not of myself: but the Father that dwelleth in me, he doeth the works.

  John 17:10 And all mine are thine, and thine are mine; and I am glorified in them.

- As sending the Spirit, equally with the Father.

  John 14:16 And I will pray the Father, and he shall give you another Comforter, that he may abide with you for ever;

  John 15:26 But when the Comforter is come, whom I will send unto you from the Father, *even* the Spirit of truth, which proceedeth from the Father, he shall testify of me:

- As entitled to equal honor with the Father.

John 5:23 That all *men* should honour the Son, even as they honour the Father. He that honoureth not the Son honoureth not the Father which hath sent him.

- As Owner of all things, equally with the Father.

John 16:15 All things that the Father hath are mine: therefore said I, that he shall take of mine, and shall shew *it* unto you.

- As unrestricted by the law of the sabbath, equally with the Father.

John 5:17 But Jesus answered them, My Father worketh hitherto, and I work.

- As the Source of grace, equally with the Father.

1 Thessalonians 3:11 Now God himself and our Father, and our Lord Jesus Christ, direct our way unto you.

2 Thessalonians 2:16-17 Now our Lord Jesus Christ himself, and God, even our Father, which hath loved us, and hath given *us* everlasting consolation and good hope through grace, Comfort your hearts, and stablish you in every good word and work.

- As unsearchable, equally with the Father.

Proverbs 30:4 Who hath ascended up into heaven, or descended? who hath gathered the wind in his fists? who hath bound the waters in a garment? who hath established all the ends of the earth? what *is* his name, and what *is* his son's name, if thou canst tell?

Matthew 11:27 All things are delivered unto me of my Father: and no man knoweth the Son, but the Father; neither knoweth any man the Father, save the Son, and *he* to whomsoever the Son will reveal *him*.

- As Creator of all things.

  Isaiah 40:28 Hast thou not known? hast thou not heard, *that* the everlasting God, the LORD, the Creator of the ends of the earth, fainteth not, neither is weary? *there is* no searching of his understanding.

  John 1:3 All things were made by him; and without him was not any thing made that was made.

  Colossians 1:16 For by him were all things created, that are in heaven, and that are in earth, visible and invisible, whether *they be* thrones, or dominions, or principalities, or powers: all things were created by him, and for him:

  Hebrews 1:2 Hath in these last days spoken unto us by *his* Son, whom he hath appointed heir of all things, by whom also he made the worlds;

- As Supporter and Preserver of all things.

  Nehemiah 9:6 Thou, *even* thou, *art* LORD alone; thou hast made heaven, the heaven of heavens, with all their host, the earth, and all *things* that *are* therein, the seas, and all that *is* therein, and thou preservest them all; and the host of heaven worshippeth thee.

  Colossians 1:17 And he is before all things, and by him all things consist.

  Hebrews 1:3 Who being the brightness of *his* glory, and the express image of his person, and upholding all things by the word of his power, when he had by himself purged our sins, sat down on the right hand of the Majesty on high;

- As possessed of the fulness of the God head.

  Colossians 2:9 For in him dwelleth all the fulness of the Godhead bodily.

Hebrews 1:3 Who being the brightness of *his* glory, and the express image of his person, and upholding all things by the word of his power, when he had by himself purged our sins, sat down on the right hand of the Majesty on high;

- As raising the dead.

John 5:21 For as the Father raiseth up the dead, and quickeneth *them*; even so the Son quickeneth whom he will.

John 6:40 And this is the will of him that sent me, that every one which seeth the Son, and believeth on him, may have everlasting life: and I will raise him up at the last day.

John 6:54 Whoso eateth my flesh, and drinketh my blood, hath eternal life; and I will raise him up at the last day.

- As raising Himself from the dead.

John 2:19 Jesus answered and said unto them, Destroy this temple, and in three days I will raise it up.

John 10:18 No man taketh it from me, but I lay it down of myself. I have power to lay it down, and I have power to take it again. This commandment have I received of my Father.

- As Eternal.

Isaiah 9:6 For unto us a child is born, unto us a son is given: and the government shall be upon his shoulder: and his name shall be called Wonderful, Counsellor, The mighty God, The everlasting Father, The Prince of Peace.

Micah 5:2 But thou, Bethlehem Ephratah, *though* thou be little among the thousands of Judah, *yet* out of thee shall he come forth unto me *that is* to be ruler in Israel; whose goings forth *have been* from of old, from everlasting.

John 1:1 In the beginning was the Word, and the Word was with God, and the Word was God.

Colossians 1:17 And he is before all things, and by him all things consist.

Hebrews 1:8-10 But unto the Son *he saith*, Thy throne, O God, *is* for ever and ever: a sceptre of righteousness *is* the sceptre of thy kingdom. Thou hast loved righteousness, and hated iniquity; therefore God, *even* thy God, hath anointed thee with the oil of gladness above thy fellows. And, Thou, Lord, in the beginning hast laid the foundation of the earth; and the heavens are the works of thine hands:

Revelation 1:8 I am Alpha and Omega, the beginning and the ending, saith the Lord, which is, and which was, and which is to come, the Almighty.

- As Omnipresent.

Matthew 18:20 For where two or three are gathered together in my name, there am I in the midst of them.

Matthew 28:20 Teaching them to observe all things whatsoever I have commanded you: and, lo, I am with you alway, *even* unto the end of the world. Amen.

John 3:13 And no man hath ascended up to heaven, but he that came down from heaven, *even* the Son of man which is in heaven.

- As Omnipotent.

Psalms 45:3 Gird thy sword upon *thy* thigh, O *most* mighty, with thy glory and thy majesty.

Philippians 3:21 Who shall change our vile body, that it may be fashioned like unto his glorious body, according to the working whereby he is able even to subdue all things unto himself.

Revelation 1:8 I am Alpha and Omega, the beginning and the ending, saith the Lord, which is, and which was, and which is to come, the Almighty.

- As Omniscient.

John 16:30 Now are we sure that thou knowest all things, and needest not that any man should ask thee: by this we believe that thou camest forth from God.

John 21:17 He saith unto him the third time, Simon, *son* of Jonas, lovest thou me? Peter was grieved because he said unto him the third time, Lovest thou me? And he said unto him, Lord, thou knowest all things; thou knowest that I love thee. Jesus saith unto him, Feed my sheep.

- As discerning the thoughts of the heart.

1 Kings 8:39 Then hear thou in heaven thy dwelling place, and forgive, and do, and give to every man according to his ways, whose heart thou knowest; (for thou, *even* thou only, knowest the hearts of all the children of men;)

Luke 5:22 But when Jesus perceived their thoughts, he answering said unto them, What reason ye in your hearts?

Ezekiel 11:5 And the Spirit of the LORD fell upon me, and said unto me, Speak; Thus saith the LORD; Thus have ye said, O house of Israel: for I know the things that come into your mind, *every one of* them.

John 2:24-25 But Jesus did not commit himself unto them, because he knew all *men*, And needed not that any should testify of man: for he knew what was in man.

- As unchangeable.

  Malachi 3:6 For I *am* the LORD, I change not; therefore ye sons of Jacob are not consumed.

  Hebrews 1:12 And as a vesture shalt thou fold them up, and they shall be changed: but thou art the same, and thy years shall not fail.

  Hebrews 13:8 Jesus Christ the same yesterday, and to day, and for ever.

- As having power to forgive sins.

  Colossians 3:13 Forbearing one another, and forgiving one another, if any man have a quarrel against any: even as Christ forgave you, so also *do* ye.

  Mark 2:7 Why doth this *man* thus speak blasphemies? who can forgive sins but God only?

  Mark 2:10 But that ye may know that the Son of man hath power on earth to forgive sins, (he saith to the sick of the palsy,)

- As Giver of pastors to the Church.

  Jeremiah 3:15 And I will give you pastors according to mine heart, which shall feed you with knowledge and understanding.

  Ephesians 4:11-13 And he gave some, apostles; and some, prophets; and some, evangelists; and some, pastors and teachers; For the perfecting of the saints, for the work of the ministry, for the edifying of the body of Christ: Till we all come in the unity of the faith, and of the knowledge of the Son of God, unto a perfect man, unto the measure of the stature of the fulness of Christ:

- As Husband of the Church.

Isaiah 54:5 For thy Maker *is* thine husband; the LORD of hosts *is* his name; and thy Redeemer the Holy One of Israel; The God of the whole earth shall he be called.

Ephesians 5:25-32 Husbands, love your wives, even as Christ also loved the church, and gave himself for it; That he might sanctify and cleanse it with the washing of water by the word, That he might present it to himself a glorious church, not having spot, or wrinkle, or any such thing; but that it should be holy and without blemish. So ought men to love their wives as their own bodies. He that loveth his wife loveth himself. For no man ever yet hated his own flesh; but nourisheth and cherisheth it, even as the Lord the church: . . .

Isaiah 62:5 For *as* a young man marrieth a virgin, *so* shall thy sons marry thee: and *as* the bridegroom rejoiceth over the bride, *so* shall thy God rejoice over thee.

Revelation 21:2 And I John saw the holy city, new Jerusalem, coming down from God out of heaven, prepared as a bride adorned for her husband.

Revelation 21:9 And there came unto me one of the seven angels which had the seven vials full of the seven last plagues, and talked with me, saying, Come hither, I will shew thee the bride, the Lamb's wife.

- As the object of divine worship.

Acts 7:59 And they stoned Stephen, calling upon *God*, and saying, Lord Jesus, receive my spirit.

2 Corinthians 12:8-9 For this thing I besought the Lord thrice, that it might depart from me. And he said unto me, My grace is sufficient for thee: for my strength is made perfect in weakness.

Most gladly therefore will I rather glory in my infirmities, that the power of Christ may rest upon me.

- As the object of faith.

Psalms 2:12 Kiss the Son, lest he be angry, and ye perish *from* the way, when his wrath is kindled but a little. Blessed *are* all they that put their trust in him.

1 Peter 2:6 Wherefore also it is contained in the scripture, Behold, I lay in Sion a chief corner stone, elect, precious: and he that believeth on him shall not be confounded.

Jeremiah 17:5 Thus saith the LORD; Cursed *be* the man that trusteth in man, and maketh flesh his arm, and whose heart departeth from the LORD.

Jeremiah 17:7 Blessed *is* the man that trusteth in the LORD, and whose hope the LORD is.

- As God, He redeems and purifies the Church to Himself.

Revelation 5:9 And they sung a new song, saying, Thou art worthy to take the book, and to open the seals thereof: for thou wast slain, and hast redeemed us to God by thy blood out of every kindred, and tongue, and people, and nation;

Titus 2:14 Who gave himself for us, that he might redeem us from all iniquity, and purify unto himself a peculiar people, zealous of good works.

- As God, He presents the Church to Himself.

Ephesians 5:27 That he might present it to himself a glorious church, not having spot, or wrinkle, or any such thing; but that it should be holy and without blemish.

Jude 1:24-25 Now unto him that is able to keep you from falling, and to present *you* faultless before the presence of his glory with exceeding joy, To the only wise God our Saviour, *be* glory and majesty, dominion and power, both now and ever. Amen.

- Saints live to Him as God.

Romans 6:11 Likewise reckon ye also yourselves to be dead indeed unto sin, but alive unto God through Jesus Christ our Lord.

Galatians 2:19 For I through the law am dead to the law, that I might live unto God.

2 Corinthians 5:15 And *that* he died for all, that they which live should not henceforth live unto themselves, but unto him which died for them, and rose again.

- Acknowledged by His Apostles.

John 20:28 And Thomas answered and said unto him, My Lord and my God.

- Acknowledged by the Old Testament saints.

Genesis 17:1 And when Abram was ninety years old and nine, the LORD appeared to Abram, and said unto him, I *am* the Almighty God; walk before me, and be thou perfect.

Genesis 48:15 And he blessed Joseph, and said, God, before whom my fathers Abraham and Isaac did walk, the God which fed me all my life long unto this day,

Genesis 32:24-30 And Jacob was left alone; and there wrestled a man with him until the breaking of the day. And when he saw that he prevailed not against him, he touched the hollow of his thigh; and the hollow of Jacob's thigh was out of joint, as he wrestled with him. And he said, Let me go, for the day breaketh. And he said, I will not let thee go, except thou bless me. And he said unto him, What *is* thy name? And he said, Jacob. And he said, Thy name shall be called no more Jacob, but Israel: for as a prince hast thou power with God and with men, and hast prevailed . . . .

Hosea 12:3-5 He took his brother by the heel in the womb, and by his strength he had power with God: Yea, he had power over the angel, and prevailed: he wept, and made supplication unto him: he found him *in* Bethel, and there he spake with us; Even the LORD God of hosts; the LORD *is* his memorial.

Judges 6:22-24 And when Gideon perceived that he *was* an angel of the LORD, Gideon said, Alas, O Lord GOD! for because I have seen an angel of the LORD face to face. And the LORD said unto him, Peace *be* unto thee; fear not: thou shalt not die. Then Gideon built an altar there unto the LORD, and called it Jehovahshalom: unto this day it *is* yet in Ophrah of the Abiezrites.

Judges 13:21-22 But the angel of the LORD did no more appear to Manoah and to his wife. Then Manoah knew that he *was* an angel of the LORD. And Manoah said unto his wife, We shall surely die, because we have seen God.

These passages were assembled by Reverend to teach about Christ's Deity in *The New Topical Textbook*, edited by R. A. Torrey, published 1897.

The powerful truth and the powerful conclusion that can be drown based on the evidence provided by the passages above will be that there is Only One God, He is the Lord Jesus Christ, the Lord is God as He said He is [John 8:24]. The Lord Jesus Christ is God as the Scriptures instruct us. As we can also see, Scriptures cannot be wrong.

- Other verses to consider in the discussions about Christ's Deity include the following:

    "And without controversy great is the mystery of godliness: GOD was manifest in the FLESH,—1 Timothy 3:16

    "But unto the SON he saith,—Hebrews 1:8, 10

"I and my Father are ONE."—Jesus Christ, John 10:30

God is one: Hear, O Israel: The LORD our God is one LORD. Deuteronomy 6:4

Jesus and God are one: I and my Father are one. John 10:30

> In the beginning was the Word, and the Word was *with God*, and the *Word was God* . . . All things were made by him . . . He was in the world, and the world was made by him, and the world knew him not . . . And the *Word was made flesh*, and dwelt among us John 1:1, 3, 10, 14

> Jesus saith . . . he that hath seen me hath seen the Father; and how *sayest* thou then, Shew us the Father? John 14:9

> For there are three that bear record in heaven, the Father, the Word, and the Holy Ghost: and *these three are one.* 1 John 5:7

The following lines show that the Lord Jesus Christ is God. As I already mentioned, I learned from other scholars and I presented the Scriptures with some modifications. These are passages from the word of God, not an individual's writings:

Activities and Conclusive Remarks

1. Now, if you believe in God, do you also believe that the Almighty God, Creator of the universe is the Lord Jesus Christ?

_____

_____

_____

_____

2) If you believe the Lord Jesus Christ is God the Creator, which verse or verses of the Scriptures clearly has or have convinced you that the Almighty God is the Lord Jesus Christ?

_____

_____

_____

_____

3) What other passages from the Scriptures would you like to share with others in order to point them to the Deity of the Lord Jesus Christ, His Power and His sovereignty?

_____

_____

_____

_____

CONCLUSION

I am the Living One; I was dead, and behold I am alive for ever and ever! And I hold the keys of death and Hades [Revelation 8:18].

[16] And without controversy great is the mystery of godliness:
God[c] was manifested in the flesh,
Justified in the Spirit,
Seen by angels,
Preached among the Gentiles,
Believed on in the world,
Received up in glory [I Timothy 3:16].

In the discussions about Christ's Deity, few facts become clear. There is Only One God and His name is the Lord Jesus Christ, The Lord Jesus is God our Creator because God calls Him God [Hebrews 1:1-6], in Him dwelt the fullness of deity: For God was pleased to have all his fullness dwell in him,… [Colossians 1:19]. The Lord Jesus Christ is God Almighty [Revelation 8:1]. To highlight many powerful arguments, *Christ' Deity: The Deity of the Lord Jesus Christ; Truth, Myth and Challenges* considers passages from various versions including New International Version and King James. Learning that there is Only One God and that the Lord Jesus Christ is God of the Old Testament and God of the New Testament is a blessing because the Lord Jesus Christ gives salvation:

Whoever eats my flesh and drinks my blood has eternal life, and I will raise them up at the last day [John 6:54]; 58 This is the bread that came down from heaven. Your ancestors ate manna and died, but whoever feeds on this bread will live forever." [John 6:58]

God is the Great Shepherd [Ezekiel 34:11-17; 23-29] and [John 10:11].

Many powerful passages from the Holy Bible clear teach us that the LORD Jesus Christ is God, our Creator. Among those Scriptures are the following: [2 Peter 1:1].

The Lord Jesus Christ invites everyone to invite Him in the heart [Revelation [3:20].

The Lord Jesus Christ is God, our Creator. He created the Heavens and the earth. And He created everything in the world. The Lord Jesus Christ created you and me. In Him dwells all Deity. The Lord created everything on earth [Colossians 1:1-15].

There is Only One God, the Creator of the heavens and the earth and Scriptures teach us that He is the LORD Jesus Christ and that He came to earth to save His people from sins sins [Matthew 1:21]. There is evidence to God's existence and the LORD's Jesus Christ Deity as God, our Creator.

Scriptures instruct us about God's existence, His power to create and Scriptures also teach us about the love of God and tell us that His Name is the Lord Jesus Christ.

Scriptures teach us who God is: The Word, the Beginning and the End, the First and the Last; the Alpha and the Omega: [8] "I am the Alpha and the Omega," says the Lord God, "who is, and who was, and who is to come, the Almighty" [Revelation 1:8].

We have learned that several Scriptures in the Word of God teach us that the Lord Jesus Christ is God as we saw in tables of juxtaposed verses from the Old Testament and from the New Testament. Scriptures are the inspired of God and we are to believe in God and obey the Lord.

Remarkable facts such as the knowledge of people's thoughts and raising the dead from death clearly testify to the Deity of the LORD Jesus Christ as God the Creator.

Some remarkable factors in the discussions of the Deity of the LORD Jesus Christ is the Lord's ability to speak to the nature and the nature obeys Him, opening the eyes of the blind only by touching them and more fascinating raising the dead and knowing peoples' hidden thoughts and knowing what is inside of people's hearts.

As we have learned from the Word of God, several Scriptures instruct us that there is Only One God and the LORD Jesus Christ is God as Scriptures teach us in the following passages:

- *"Hear, O Israel! Yahweh is our God, Yahweh is one!"* [Deuteronomy 6:4].

- *"You are great, O Lord God; for there is none like You, and there is no God besides You"* [2 Samuel 7:22].

- [29]"The most important one," answered Jesus, "is this: 'Hear, O Israel: The Lord our God, the Lord is one.[c] [30] Love the Lord your God with all your heart and with all your soul and with all your mind and with all your strength.'[f] [31] The second is this: 'Love your neighbor as yourself.'[g] There is no commandment greater than these."

Some people doubt God's existence and some even do not believe that He is the LORD Jesus Christ. WHO do you think? As already discussed, some people deny God's existence and doubt God. But, many believe in God and many people are aware that God, our Creator is the Lord Jesus Christ. C.S Lewis states that Jesus Christ could be a liar, a lunatic, or God. He elaborated on His thoughts and concluded that it is impossible with the Lord's character to be a liar or to be a lunatic; therefore the LORD Jesus Christ is who He claimed to be. Who do you think, the LORD Jesus Christ Is?

God reveals Himself when we seek him with all our hearts and God gives the Holy Spirit to he who asks:

- [Matthew 7: 7-12].
- [Hebrews 11:6].

By faith we understand that the world was created by God; without faith it is impossible to please God [Hebrews 11:6].

The LORD Jesus teaches that if we do not believe that He is the ONE He Says that He is, we will perish: [John 8:24].

There will be judgment on the last Day, if we do not believe in the Lord Jesus Christ we will perish. The LORD said: Here I am! I stand at the door and knock. If anyone hears my voice and opens the door, I will come in and eat with that person, and they with me [Revelation 3:20]

The Lord says: Jesus answered, "I am the way and the truth and the life [John 14:6].

Elsewhere the Lord says that he will never reject those whoever comes to Him: [John 6:37].

And the lord says: [Revelation 3:20].

The Lord Jesus Christ asks His Disciples: Who do you think I am?

Today this question is asked to you. Who do You Think the LORD Jesus Christ Is?

The Lord says: [Revelation3:20]. Another important passage to consider is [Romans 10:13].

In conclusion, a juxtaposition of passages of the Scriptures such as a table of juxtaposed Scriptures by Rev. Matt Slick is worth recalling among several others.

Jesus is God

by Matt Slick

"You are my witnesses," declares the LORD, "and my servant whom I have chosen, so that you may know and believe me and understand that I am he. Before me no god was formed, nor will there be one after me," (Isaiah 43:10).

JESUS	IS	GOD, "YAHWEH"
John 1:3, "Through him all things were made; without him nothing was made that has been made."		Job 33:4, "The Spirit of God has made me; the breath of the Almighty gives me life."
Col. 1:16-17, "For by him all things were created: things in heaven and on earth, visible and invisible, whether thrones or powers or rulers or authorities; all things were created by him and for him. He is before all things, and in him all things hold together."	**Creator**	Isaiah 40:28, "Do you not know? Have you not heard? The LORD is the everlasting God, the Creator of the ends of the earth. He will not grow tired or weary, and his understanding no one can fathom."
Rev. 1:17, "When I saw him, I fell at his feet as though dead. Then he placed his right hand on me and said: 'Do not be afraid. I am the First and the Last.'"		Isaiah 41:4, "Who has done this and carried it through, calling forth the generations from the beginning? I, the LORD—with the first of them and with the last—I am he."
Rev. 2:8, "To the angel of the church in Smyrna write: These are the words of him who is the First and the Last, who died and came to life again."	**First and Last**	Isaiah 44:6, "This is what the LORD says—Israel's King and Redeemer, the LORD Almighty: I am the first and I am the last; apart from me there is no God."
Rev. 22:13, "I am the Alpha and the Omega, the First and the Last, the Beginning and the End."		Isaiah 48:12, "Listen to me, O Jacob, Israel, whom I have called: I am he; I am the first and I am the last."

John 8:24, "Therefore I said to you that you will die in your sins; for if you do not believe that I am He, you will die in your sins." (NKJV)

Exodus 3:14, "God said to Moses, "I AM WHO I AM. This is what you are to say to the Israelites: 'I AM has sent me to you.'"

John 8:58, "I tell you the truth," Jesus answered, "before Abraham was born, I am!" See Exodus 3:14

Isaiah 43:10, "You are my witnesses," declares the LORD, "and my servant whom I have chosen, so that you may know and believe me and understand that I am he. Before me no god was formed, nor will there be one after me."

John 13:19, "I am telling you now before it happens, so that when it does happen you will believe that I am He."

I AM

"ego eimi"

See also Deut. 32:39

2 Tim. 4:1, "In the presence of God and of Christ Jesus, who will judge the living and the dead, and in view of his appearing and his kingdom, I give you this charge . . ."

Joel 3:12, "Let the nations be roused; let them advance into the Valley of Jehoshaphat, for there I will sit to judge all the nations on every side."

2 Cor. 5:10, "For we must all appear before the judgment seat of Christ, that each one may receive what is due him for the things done while in the body, whether good or bad."

Judge

Rom. 14:10, "You, then, why do you judge your brother? Or why do you look down on your brother? For we will all stand before God's judgment seat."

Matt. 2:2, ". . . Where is the one who has been born king of the Jews? We saw his star in the east and have come to worship him."

Luke 23:3, "So Pilate asked Jesus, "Are you the king of the Jews?" "Yes, it is as you say," Jesus replied."

See also John 19:21

King

Jer. 10:10, "But the LORD is the true God; he is the living God, the eternal King. When he is angry, the earth trembles; the nations cannot endure his wrath."

Isaiah 44:6-8, "This is what the LORD says—Israel's King and Redeemer, the LORD Almighty: I am the first and I am the last; apart from me there is no God."

See also Psalm 47

Psalm 27:1, "The LORD is my light and my salvation—whom shall I fear?"

John 8:12, "When Jesus spoke again to the people, he said, "I am the light of the world. Whoever follows me will never walk in darkness, but will have the light of life."

Luke 2:32, "a light for revelation to the Gentiles and for glory to your people Israel."

See also John 1:7-9

Light

Isaiah 60:20, "our sun will never set again, and your moon will wane no more; the LORD will be your everlasting light, and your days of sorrow will end."

1 John 1:5, "God is light; in him there is no darkness at all."

1 Cor. 10:4, ". . . for they drank from the spiritual rock that accompanied them, and that rock was Christ."

See also 1 Pet. 2:4-8.

Rock

Deut. 32:4, "He is the Rock, his works are perfect, and all his ways are just. A faithful God who does no wrong, upright and just is he."

See also 2 Sam. 22:32 and Isaiah 17:10.

John 4:42, "They said to the woman, 'We no longer believe just because of what you said; now we have heard for ourselves, and we know that this man really is the Savior of the world.'"

1 John 4:14, "And we have seen and testify that the Father has sent his Son to be the Savior of the world."

Savior

Isaiah 43:3, "For I am the LORD, your God, the Holy One of Israel, your Savior"

Isaiah 45:21, ". . . And there is no God apart from me, a righteous God and a Savior; there is none but me."

John 10:11, "I am the good shepherd. The good shepherd lays down his life for the sheep."

Heb. 13:20, "May the God of peace, who through the blood of the eternal covenant brought back from the dead our Lord Jesus, that great Shepherd of the sheep,"

Shepherd

Psalm 23:1, "The LORD is my shepherd, I shall not be in want."

Isaiah 40:11, "He tends his flock like a shepherd: He gathers the lambs in his arms and carries them close to his heart; he gently leads those that have young."

See also John 10:14,16; 1 Pet. 2:25

Unless otherwise noted, all quotations are from the NASB.

[16] Beyond all question, the mystery from which true godliness springs is great:

He appeared in the flesh,
was vindicated by the Spirit,[d]
was seen by angels,
was preached among the nations,
was believed on in the world,
was taken up in glory[I Timothy 3:16].

REFERENCES

The Holy Bible, New International Versions 1984.

C.S. Lewis: Mere Christianity. Harper San Francisco, A division of Harper Collins Publishers 1980.

Matt Slick: Jesus is God. Article from the Internet. CARM. 2010. Bible verses that show Jesus is Divine. Article from the Internet. CARM. 2010.

The Miracles of Jesus. Article from the Internet. CARM. 2010.

Is Jesus or God the Creator of all things? Article from the Internet. CARM. 2010.

Jesus' Two Natures: God and Man. Article from the Internet. CARM. 2010. Is Jesus or God the Creator of all things? The Miracles of Jesus Article from the Internet. CARM. 2010.

R. A. Torrey: The New Topical Textbook, 1897.

Annie Ngana Mundeke: The Gift Everyone Needs. Publish America. 2009. US.

Phillip E. Johnson. 1997 Defeating Darwinism By Open Minds. Intervarsity Press. United States of America

Perloff James. 2003. *The Case Against Darwin: Why the Evidence Should Be Examined. Refuse Books. The United States of America*

ABOUT THE WRITER

Dr. Annie Ngana-Mundeke is a cultural Anthropologist, she is a college professor and she is a writer. She was born in a Christian home from Christian parents and she grew up in a Christian family with her brothers and sisters. Annie accepted the Lord Jesus Christ as her personal Savior when she was young. She thanks God for being the provider, *Jehovah Jireh* [Genesis 22:8, 14].

Some critical events that have marked her life include the loss of her beloved younger sister Veronica, who died very young, before she attended pre-school. The loss of her father when she was in high school, following by the murder of her beloved elder brother Tshibamba André (Chico), who was kidnapped in the middle of the night and beaten to death before he was brutally murdered by people he did not know. However, the thought that there is God, Who sees, *El-Roi* [Genesis 16:13]; who conquered death [John 2:19; I Corinthians 15:55-56], the Almighty *EL-Shaddai* [Genesis 28:3]; the Alpha and the Omega [Revelation 1:8]; and the Judge brings peace, comfort, and hope to Sylvia and her family.